The gospels record that Jesus saw individuals through eyes of compassion, loved people where they were, and touched them with unconditional love. That's what Coffee Break is all about, and this book powerfully describes the reality of lives that have been changed through its ministry. Highly inspiring, scripturally sound, and deeply motivating, *Touching Lives with Love* reveals how women committed to Christ can impact lives with God's love.

Carol Kent
Speaker and Author of *Becoming a Woman of Influence*

Transformation requires community—a place where truth and grace encounter love and nurture. These powerful stories are moving examples of how and where such transformation takes place. Read them and allow these stories to become your own.

Bill Donahue
Vice President, Small Group Ministries
Willow Creek Association

I have long admired the Coffee Break ministry for its emphasis on the power of God's Word, the power of prayer, and the power of Christ's love mediated through small groups. Now Marie Van Antwerpen has compiled real life stories of how God's grace has touched the lives of countless women through this vital and important ministry. I am grateful that she wrote it—you will be too.

Rebecca Manley Pippert
Author of *Out of the Salt Shaker* and *A Heart Like His*

I was particularly touched to read the testimonies of women who were invited to Coffee Break as "seekers." Why can't we as a universal church do this more often? The answer: We can, and Coffee Break will help! I would recommend *Touching Lives with Love* to anyone who wants to know for sure that there is a God who cares about them and that this God's greatest desire is to be found. These stories are full of the fingerprints of God's work.

Russ Robinson
Director of Ministries and Small Groups
Willow Creek Community Church

The Coffee Break ministry embodies my own personal mission statement: To touch the heart of God and inspire the whole world to do the same. It is obvious in reading these stories that Coffee Break has touched God's heart by transforming lives through God's love. I celebrate with you!

Gwen McVicker
Servant Leader, B.C. Prayer and Evangelism Network
Coordinator, AD 2000
Canadian Christian Women United

Reading this book is like enjoying a wonderful dessert. At first taste, it tells the inspirational story of a ministry you want to start in your church tomorrow morning. Let it digest awhile, and it dawns on you that you have just read one of the finest texts on modern evangelism, with nuggets and morsels of wisdom layered in every life-changing story. Finally, after you sit back and sip a cup of coffee, this book moves you to worship—it makes you want to stand up and cheer for God.

David Stark
Small Group Consultant
Church Innovations, Inc.

Having spoken at the Coffee Break international convention as well as at local gatherings of Coffee Break groups, I was thrilled to read this marvelous collection of stories about real women and their life-changing encounters through this ministry. Each person's journey is not only an inspiration, but also a challenge to share Christ's love and hope with all those around us.

Lucinda Secrest McDowell
Speaker and Author of *Quilts from Heaven*

Marie Van Antwerpen

Touching Lives with Love

CRC Publications
Grand Rapids, Michigan

Cover illustration: Kent Eimers Photography

Unless otherwise indicated, the Scripture quotations in this publication are from the HOLY BIBLE, NEW INTERNATIONAL VERSION, © 1973, 1978, 1984, International Bible Society. Used by permission of Zondervan Bible Publishers.

Coffee Break: Touching Lives with Love, © 2000 by CRC Publications, 2850 Kalamazoo Ave. SE, Grand Rapids, MI 49560. All rights reserved. With the exception of brief excerpts for review purposes, no part of this book may be reproduced in any manner whatsoever without written permission from the publisher. Printed in the United States of America on recycled paper. ✺

We welcome your comments. Call 1-800-333-8300 or e-mail us at editors@crcpublications.org.

Library of Congress Cataloging-in-Publication Data
Van Antwerpen, Marie, 1938-
    Coffee break: touching lives with love / Marie Van Antwerpen.
       p.   cm.
    ISBN 1-56212-552-4
    1. Christian biography. I. Title.
BR1700.2.V36 2000
242—dc21
                                       00-022945

10 9 8 7 6 5 4 3 2 1

Contents

Foreword 8
Pressing on Toward the Goal 12
Comfort from Above 16
Free at Last 20
Healing for the Heart 24
A New Self 28
Like a Child 32
Walking in the Light 36
Teach Me Your Paths 40
Chosen by the Father 44
The Good News About Jesus 48
Rest for the Weary 52
Lord, Hear My Cry 56
God's Perfect Plan 60
Open Our Eyes, Lord 64
Sharing the Riches of Christ 68
Seek and You Will Find 72
Living Water for a Thirsty Soul 76
A New Song 80
Trust in the Lord 84
Fear Not, You Are Mine 88
Touching Lives with Love 92
Afterword 96

Foreword

Was it really thirty years ago that it all began? It's hard to believe. So much has happened in our lives, as well as in the ministry of Coffee Break. Yet the feelings that well up and the memories that leap to mind as we reflect on that three-decade-old beginning are fresh and real.

Four words summarize that wonder-filled experience for us: *call, prayer, joy,* and *journey.* Branded into our hearts by the Spirit of the living God, they highlight for us what gave birth to Coffee Break—not only in our lives and in the life of Peace Church, but also in the lives of so many who subsequently became a part of the Coffee Break family. Some of their stories are beautifully told in this volume.

Like the biblical story of Abraham, the father of all believers, the story of Coffee Break begins with a *call.* First came the call that brought together a congregation and a pastor. In the late 1960s a small group of families felt called to begin a new church in the community of South Holland, Illinois. They had hopes and dreams of birthing more than just another church in the community. The goal was to reach their fast-growing, increasingly secular suburban community in a way no other church had done before. God led this group to call Rev. Alvin Vander Griend to become the first pastor of Peace Church.

Meanwhile, Neva Evenhouse was hearing a call as well. Active in the founding of Peace Church, she was experiencing an increasing sense of restlessness. It wasn't just a matter of making use of the extra time she had now that her youngest child had started school. Rather, it was a deep and intense desire to be involved in and for the ministry of Peace Church. How, what, or why—she had no idea. She knew only that it was a deeply felt call. A good pastor recognizes when a parishioner is being called. So God brought together these calls, and in 1970 Coffee Break/Story Hour was born.

A good pastor also encourages *prayer* as the ministry that gives life and health to all the other ministries in the church. So prayer was a vital part of Coffee Break from the very beginning. Again and again we stood amazed at the marvelous ways in which God led us to pray and then answered our prayers—even with some closed doors. Neither of us can forget the day the first Bible study group met at Neva's home. Several women assured us they were coming. And not a soul came! God knew that Neva had to cut her eyeteeth on some one-to-one Bible studies first. These early lessons in prayer were and continue to be the life-blood of the Coffee Break ministry.

The *joy* we experienced was unbounded. Sometimes we felt the joy of watching the Holy Spirit at work through a given week's discussion. At other times we were overwhelmed by joy because of our unbelievably rapid growth. (Remember that no one showed up at our first Bible study.) Often it was the joy of a biblical discovery that touched our lives. But the greatest joy of all was to witness—over and over and over again—people coming to know Jesus Christ as their own Lord and Savior, and then to watch the Word take root in their lives. Sometimes we felt we could hardly contain the joy!

Perhaps the umbrella word in this story is *journey*. So we're back to Abraham again. Abraham was called out on a journey of faith. We set out on that same journey of faith in following Jesus, who calls us to be his fellow travelers. In a very real sense all of our life is a journey, from the beginning of our days until their end. But the journey of faith takes form in consciously listening to God's call, in following Jesus' footsteps, in sensing the Spirit's leading, and in experiencing the growth of the Spirit's gifts in our own lives.

Coffee Break was and is an important part of our individual faith journeys. It was and is an important part of the journey of the Christian Reformed Church, as well as that of other churches and denominations. Indeed, the journeys of many, many persons and families and churches (some of which are included in this book) were blessed and made fruitful by the gift of Coffee Break. For that we are profoundly thankful.

To God be the glory!

Neva Evenhouse
Alvin Vander Griend
Cofounders of Coffee Break/Story Hour

Pressing on Toward the Goal

Not that I have already obtained all this, or have already been made perfect, but I press on. . . . Forgetting what is behind and straining toward what is ahead, I press on toward the goal to win the prize for which God has called me heavenward in Christ Jesus.

—Philippians 3:12-14

Tucked away in the Santa Cruz Mountains of California is the beautiful conference center Mount Hermon. It is a place of rest and fellowship for thousands who come for a few days or a week of spiritual refreshment and renewal. Ancient redwoods tower above the buildings, and well-worn paths provide access to forest and stream.

Growing up in Northern California, it was my privilege to attend Mount Hermon Bible Conference during the last week of every summer. This family camp provided a wonderful framework for getting to know God through his Word and his world. As a young girl, though, my focus was on my friends and the activities we'd enjoy. We endured the inspirational meetings and speakers for the fun that would follow.

One summer morning, however, my perspective changed. I remember the experience as if it were yesterday. The speaker had a passion for young people. That morning Rev. Schaal challenged us with the question, "Is God calling *you* to full-time service in his kingdom?" Although I was sitting toward the back of the full auditorium, I felt as if I were the only one in the room. It seemed that Rev. Schaal was speaking directly to me, and my heart burned. Can you identify with that feeling? Have you ever felt that words written on a page or delivered in a message were aimed directly at you? It's a little scary, isn't it?

Later I left my friends and took a walk along the Mount Hermon trails—alone. As I walked, I talked to God. "Lord, what are you saying to me? Do you want me to go to Africa?" I knew I couldn't go to Africa yet; I hadn't even gone to high school. But that day, underneath the giant redwoods, I felt God's call. I could trust God to reveal the details later; after all, I was only twelve.

For the next few years completing my education took priority in my life, and God's call was put on the back burner. And when the marvelous young man I met and married did not feel "called" to missions, I believed God's plan for my life meant teaching, marriage, and motherhood. After my second child was born I felt that life had arranged itself very well. In a note to a friend, I quoted these verses from Psalm 16 to describe how I felt:

> L ORD, you have assigned me my portion and my cup;
> you have made my lot secure.
> The boundary lines have fallen for me in pleasant places;
> surely I have a delightful inheritance.

I liked how the lines of my life had been drawn, and I didn't want a thing to change. However, within a week of writing that note, tragedy entered my secure little world when my husband was diagnosed with a malignant brain tumor. As I came to grips with the seriousness of his illness, I had to wrestle with those verses from Psalm 16. Did I believe that God was in control of my life? I knew the answer was yes. God had assigned me my portion and my cup, but I certainly didn't like these newly defined lines. They were neither pleasant nor delightful. What did it mean, then, that I had "a *delightful inheritance?*" Through the nudging of the Holy Spirit, I came to realize that my inheritance was my eternal relationship with God through Christ. It would "never perish, spoil, or fade," and it would never be taken from me. Belonging to the Lord did not guarantee me freedom from pain or loss, but it did guarantee a place in heaven. That was my "delightful inheritance."

The psalms continued to provide comfort and direction during the time I cared for my disabled husband along with my infant and toddler. I often turned to David's words in Psalm 40: "I waited patiently for the L ORD; he turned to me and heard my cry. . . . He set my feet on a rock and gave me a firm place to stand." That year I discovered that spiritual growth comes from standing— standing firm to learn humility, patience, trust, and endurance.

When I was widowed a year later, I drew strength from a verse given to me years earlier at my profession of faith: "Not that I have already obtained all this, or have already been made perfect, but I press on. . . . Forgetting what is behind and straining toward what is ahead, I press on toward the goal to win the prize for which God has called me heavenward in Christ Jesus" (Phil. 3:12-14).

Was it time, I wondered, to press on toward God's call?

God's answer was clearly yes when he brought a new love into my life and provided a father for my young sons. Marriage to Bert, a pastor who shared my passion for following God's call, shaped the direction of my life, and I did "press on." Soon after, my new husband and I moved with our little family to New England to take up ministry in a "mission church." Coffee Break and Story Hour were new programs being developed just at that time, and they offered the opportunity for us to reach our community for Christ.

As I attended the initial training workshop, I knew I had found my calling. This was ministry I could do—right in my own backyard. I didn't have to go to Africa after all. It had been twenty-five years since I had walked the redwood forest trail, praying about God's call on my life. Perhaps those years had been my preparation for what lay ahead.

Coffee Break—touching lives with God's love and ours. Story Hour—introducing little ones to Jesus. I loved it, and so did the women and children in our neighborhood. So did my pastor husband, who recognized the effectiveness of this evangelism ministry. Through the study of God's Word, women and their families were coming to faith in Christ, lives were being changed, and the church was growing. Coffee Break was growing too, and a representative was needed in our area. When I answered the Coffee Break call, the door opened to a ministry that would span the next fifteen years and include serving as a regional representative for Coffee Break and Story Hour in three separate areas of the United States. As I traveled throughout the United States and Canada, I met women and children whose lives had been touched through this ministry. I often asked them to tell me their stories. And they did. These stories were wonderful testimonies to God's grace, and I wrote many of them down. "Someday," I'd say, "I'm going to write a book. A book of Coffee Break stories."

That day has come and this is the book. It is a book that celebrates God's blessings on his children through Coffee Break and Story Hour. It's a book that witnesses to the power of God's Word to change lives. It's a book about love. In writing the stories I was often moved to tears by the beautiful ways in which God works in the lives of his people. It is my prayer that as you read these stories, you will be moved to "press on toward the goal to win the prize for which God has called you in Christ Jesus."

Prayer

Lord God, thank you for the story of love that we find in the written Word. Thank you that your love story has transformed my life story. Give me the grace to share that touch of love with all I meet as I press on toward the goal in life. In Jesus' name, Amen.

Comfort from Above

The LORD comforts his people

and will have compassion on his afflicted ones.

But Zion said, "The LORD has forsaken me,

the Lord has forgotten me."

Can a mother forget the baby at her breast

and have no compassion on the child she has borne?

Though she may forget,

I will not forget you!

See, I have engraved you on the palms of my hands.

—Isaiah 49:13-16

*Sometimes I feel like a motherless child.
Sometimes I feel like a motherless child,
a long way from home.*

The words to the song kept floating through Karen's head. She just couldn't put them away. That's exactly how she felt—like a motherless child, a long way from home. The words were partly true; she and her husband had recently moved to a new community in the East, a long way from her childhood home and her extended family. But she wasn't motherless; her family still loved and cared about her. Karen just *felt* abandoned.

As she mulled over her feelings, Karen was interrupted by the crying of her infant daughter. She realized she had been blue ever since the baby was born. Her friends called it "postpartum depression"—Karen called it "the pits" and wondered how long it would last. The baby was several months old now; surely it was time to get beyond these sad feelings and experience some joy. "Your problems will go away if you pray more," advised her friends. And while they meant well, their advice didn't help much. It only added guilt to the blues.

To be honest, Karen wasn't praying much these days. "My prayers never seem to go beyond the ceiling anyway," she figured, "so why bother?" Whatever faith was left from her childhood was at a low ebb. Karen felt that God had abandoned her. Going to church and reading her Bible were the last things she felt like doing. All she wanted to do was give up. In her anguish she cried out, "God, how long will this last? I'm feeling so alone."

In the midst of this bleak period, Karen's husband shared his concern for Karen's well-being with a friend from work. The two men talked about ways to strengthen family relationships. This new acquaintance was attending a Bible study for men called Men's Life at a local church, and he had found it helpful to discover truths from the Bible that were relevant to his life. He knew the church offered a program for women also. Maybe Karen would find it valuable. And that was how Karen first learned about Coffee Break.

At first Karen was cynical about what Coffee Break could do for her. "It's probably just another one of those Bible studies that tells you what you should believe and lays a guilt trip on you if you don't," she told herself. But she decided it was worth a try—she could always quit if she didn't like it. At least it was something to do, and there was a nursery for her little one.

Karen soon found out that Coffee Break was different from other Bible studies she'd been to. She discovered that she could study the Bible for what it had to say *to her*. She could be a *seeker* of truth; having all the answers didn't matter. Plus she could participate on her own level. If she was having a down day, she could express that. If she doubted God's love for her or some teaching in the Bible, she could say so. No one lectured or pressured her about her "walk with the Lord." The Word of God was central to all the discussions, but there was space for people to be themselves. Coffee Break leaders and the other class members offered Karen friendship, prayer, and help at home as needed.

Karen began to feel loved and accepted as she experienced the love within her small group. She also recognized the source of this love—it came from God. Karen began to realize that God had not abandoned her. The comfort and encouragement that flowed from God through the leaders to Karen began to lift her spirits. Gradually experiencing her life as good once again, Karen knew she had turned the corner in her struggle with depression.

Do you ever feel alone—a long way from home? I do. Being married to a minister means that our family has made some major moves—coast to coast as well as places in between. Getting settled in a new home, new church, new community takes time and effort. Making new friends doesn't happen overnight; relationships require work. There have been times after a move that I'd get depressed and think, "I want to go *home*." But where was home? Was it the parsonage we had vacated a few weeks earlier? Was it the community where I was raised? Or was home where I was living right now? A small sign in my kitchen reads, "Home is where the heart is." I knew the sign was true. I was home. My heart was with my husband and family in this "new-to-me" house. But sometimes I needed more than that knowledge to feel at home in my church and community. And that's where Coffee Break came in.

Being part of a Coffee Break group has helped me, like Karen, through many transitions. The caring atmosphere of a small group provides a place for me to give and receive love. As it offers a place to be nurtured spiritually, the little group soon becomes "home." Perhaps that has been your experience too. Changes in life can make us feel alone, isolated, forgotten, or abandoned. Whether it's the birth of a child or a cross-country move, change can upset our emotional and spiritual apple carts. The warmth of a small group like Coffee Break can be just the right prescription for loneliness or feelings of abandonment. Because Coffee Break is focused on the Word of God, it is the Holy Spirit who empowers the love that the group shares. The transforming power of God's Word renews lives and brings hope and healing. Karen and I can testify to that.

If you are feeling forgotten, abandoned by friends and even by God, the words from the prophet Isaiah are for you. "Can a mother forget the baby at her breast and have no compassion on the child she has borne?" Emotional and spiritual depression may cause a human mother to neglect her child. But read a little further in the passage. "Though she may forget, I will not forget you! See, I have engraved you on the palms of my hands." God loves you enough to write your name on his hand. You are not like a motherless or fatherless child. You are loved.

Prayer

Lord, thank you for loving me so much you call me your child. Give me grace to share that love with all who feel abandoned or lonely. In Jesus, Amen.

Free at Last

Praise the LORD, O my soul;

all my inmost being, praise his holy name.

Praise the LORD, O my soul,

and forget not all his benefits—

who forgives all your sins

and heals all your diseases,

who redeems your life from the pit

and crowns you with love and compassion,

who satisfies your desires with good things

so that your youth is renewed like the eagle's.

The LORD is compassionate and gracious,

slow to anger, abounding in love.

—Psalm 103:1-5, 8

When I asked Michelle, a Canadian Coffee Break director, what her favorite Scripture was, she replied with a sparkle in her dark eyes, "I love Psalm 103. It really describes what God has done for me. That part about 'redeeming your life from the pit,' well, that's *my* story. I never get tired of praising God, for he has forgiven me, healed me, redeemed me, and he satisfies my desires. I can read Psalm 103 every day—but I didn't always feel that way." And then Michelle began to share her story with me.

Michelle grew up in what she described as "a crazy situation." For her and her brothers and sisters, life was full of insecurity and fear. Her dad was an alcoholic, and it took all of her mom's resources to cope. Instead of the love and protection they longed for, the six siblings lived with emptiness and confusion. Michelle remembers many nights as a young child cowering under the covers of her bed, trying to block out the sounds outside her bedroom, or jumping out of the bedroom windows with her brothers and sisters and hiding in the bushes until morning, when it would be safe to go back inside. Michelle's eyes filled with tears as she recalled, "I never felt secure in my home. I grew up with a hole inside of me—a hole that I desperately wanted to fill with love but didn't know how."

During her early teens that hole grew bigger, and Michelle began to seek ways to fill the void. When people paid attention to her—even when the attention was inappropriate—she felt special. Michelle spent her adolescence "looking for love in all the wrong places" and ended up feeling even emptier than before. Her teen years were filled with drinking, drugs, and promiscuity. Alcohol and drugs temporarily numbed the emptiness and pain, but their use led to even greater problems. Michelle found herself the victim of rape more than once. The hole inside of her grew larger and the emptiness more intense.

When she became pregnant while living with her boyfriend, she thought she'd finally found a way to fill that void. "This was going to be great—someone to love me, someone for me to love," she said. But she was persuaded to have an abortion, even though it seemed all wrong. "I will never forget the day I ended an innocent life." By this time she knew she needed to climb out of the pit she was in. She needed help.

Michelle decided that marriage to someone with "a normal lifestyle" would fill her emptiness and bring love and happiness into her life. When the man she hoped to marry broke off their engagement, she saw security slipping out of her hands once again. In desperation she tried to hold on to his love by attempting suicide. The holes in her heart seemed to increase. Even her eventual marriage and the birth of a child did not fill up the spaces. Though she was seeking, she wasn't finding what she needed to fill the emptiness. Her marriage soon ended in divorce, leaving her lonely and filled with longing.

The world is filled with people like Michelle who are seeking and not finding. Perhaps you can identify with Michelle's search for love and security. When we feel lost and alone it is tempting to grab for happiness regardless of the cost. Michelle discovered that drugs, alcohol, sex, even marriage and a child couldn't fill her void. Some of us have discovered that people, possessions, and power can't fill the holes in our hearts either. Our addictions may have a different name, or take a different form, but they leave us just as empty. So where do we go to be filled? There is only One who can truly fill the void in our lives, as Michelle eventually discovered.

Looking back, Michelle can see that God had been working in her life. When she met her present husband, she knew she wanted to leave her old ways behind her. "We decided we would go to church. It just seemed like the right thing to do." And that was how God began to work in their hearts. During this time an acquaintance told her about Coffee Break, and Michelle discovered how God could fill up those empty spaces and satisfy her desires with good things.

"When I first went to Coffee Break and met the other women," Michelle said, "I told myself, 'This is the life I want.' I could hardly wait for Wednesdays. The Coffee Break session always started with singing, and the music drew me right to God." Michelle began to read her Bible every day and eagerly shared what she was learning with her husband. They decided to attend the church that offered Coffee Break. It was then that Michelle realized that "studying God's Word and hanging out with other Christians was what I had been looking for all these years. I found what I had been seeking, and I felt alive, excited, happy, and filled to the brim."

As Michelle finished her story, she said, "Now do you see why Psalm 103 means so much to me? Satan had a tight grip on me for a long time, but today I am free! I am free to forgive myself. Free to forgive and love my parents. Free to forgive and love those who caused me pain. Free to celebrate the Lord. Free to serve the Lord. I am free because Christ died to set me free. I know what it means to be 'redeemed from the pit.' For the first time in my life, my desires are satisfied with good things, and I believe God has renewed the youth that I was trying to destroy. This psalm says it all for me, and I praise the Lord."

How about you? Can Psalm 103 become your personal prayer of praise as you reflect on God's love and compassion? Sometimes our sins, our diseases, and our difficulties seem overwhelmingly large. But Psalm 103 teaches us that God's love is greater than our transgressions, for God not only forgives our sins, he forgets them. What must we do to be forgiven? Repent and believe.

Prayer

Lord, I receive your love. Thank you for forgiving my sins and filling my life with compassion. Praise the Lord, O my soul. Praise the Lord. Amen.

Healing for the Heart

I the L<small>ORD</small> search the heart

and examine the mind,

to reward a man according to his conduct,

according to what his deeds deserve.

Heal me, O L<small>ORD</small>, and I will be healed;

save me and I will be saved,

for you are the one I praise.

—Jeremiah 17:10, 14

It was Wednesday morning and time for Little Lambs to begin. Linda hurried to keep up with her little son, Danny, as he ran into the church and bounded down the steps to the basement. "Hurry up, Mom," Danny called. "I want to do Play-Doh today." Linda smiled as she watched her enthusiastic son. "Wish I had his energy," she said to herself. "He certainly loves Little Lambs." Linda liked Little Lambs too. She was glad to have discovered a program where her children could get some spiritual teaching and have fun at the same time. This Elmhurst, Illinois, church provided a great experience for preschoolers, and the staff were wonderful. Linda admired the teachers' patience and love. She knew what it took to keep up with bouncy little boys like Danny.

Danny was a typical two-and-a-half-year-old, with one exception. He was born with a heart murmur. Initially the doctors and the family did not realize the seriousness of his condition, and Danny, though small for his age, had lots of energy. Then Linda noticed that the wall of his chest protruded unnaturally. A nurse as well as a mother, Linda knew something was wrong. An ultrasound and angiogram indicated a hole in Danny's enlarged heart. Open-heart surgery was scheduled for his third birthday. To complicate matters, Linda's husband lost his job right at that time, and the family felt overwhelmed. "One of the first things to cross my mind," Linda reflected, "was 'How will we pay for this surgery?'" She had lots of questions and very little faith in God.

As a child Linda had gone to church and Sunday school, but by the time she was in college she had drifted away. "My husband and I were married in a church," she said, "and for a while we went on Christmas and Easter. But we did not have a church home, and we had no relationship with God." Little Lambs was providing a connection to God, however, and Linda sensed that this was good. One day shortly before the surgery, when she picked up Danny from his class, the teacher came out to talk with her. "We are praying for Danny," the teacher told her.

"That touched my heart," Linda recalled. "Imagine. These teachers cared enough for Danny to pray for him." That simple sentence of a promise to pray was a seed planted in Linda's heart. People appreciate prayers. Parents, especially, appreciate prayers for their children.

About a week later Linda was pushing a grocery cart down the aisle of the supermarket near her home. She was deep in thought about the coming surgery. A date had been set; very soon the surgery would be a reality. Her husband still had no job, and Linda was worried. She turned the corner and almost bumped into Jane, director of the Little Lambs program. When Jane asked about Danny, Linda began to pour out her heart. Jane simply listened. She sensed that this was a "divine encounter" and knew that running into Linda was no accident.

Have you "been there, done that?" Whether you have been the one pouring out your heart or the one listening, you know that spiritual encounters can occur in the produce section or next to the dairy case. The Holy Spirit can transform the grocery store, the church parking lot, or the backyard fence into a place of spiritual healing. Linda was comforted by Jane's willingness to listen as she shared her problems, and the seeds of faith in Linda's heart were nourished.

Danny's surgery went well, and he came home to recuperate. That week Jane stopped to see him, bringing a small gift and words of encouragement. Once again Linda was the recipient of kindness given in the name of Christ. "At that point I realized that these Little Lambs leaders had a quality of care and compassion that I wanted. They had something I didn't have. I wasn't sure how to get it, but I knew it was connected with the church, and I knew I needed to find what it was."

When Danny had healed sufficiently, he returned to Little Lambs. Linda offered to be a substitute teacher for the church's program, filling in when needed. She knew it would give her the opportunity to observe the teachers in action. "Here was my chance to see these leaders up close and personal," she said. "There was love, there was patience, there was joy in the way they served. I just wanted to be around them." In time she came to recognize the source of their strength and joy. "I realized it was a spiritual thing. These women had a relationship with God that I didn't have," she said. "The love of Jesus in their hearts was the difference. That was something I had never cultivated." Linda's heart needed healing, and she prayed to the One who had the power to heal.

The hole in Danny's heart was repaired by surgery. The process was complicated and costly, but definitely worth it. Today Danny is healthy and doing well. The hole in Linda's heart needed repair also, but that transformation was provided free of charge, for Jesus had already paid the price.

Linda recognized her need for God, put her faith in Jesus as Savior, and received a transformed heart by the Holy Spirit. Today she eagerly shares her testimony. "I lived apart from Christ for a long time," she said, "but God gave me a wake-up call, and now I live in total dependence on him. I thank God for using Little Lambs to open my heart to him."

Linda's appreciation motivated her to continue helping with Little Lambs long after Danny grew out of the program. "I know the importance of providing this outreach to our community," she stated. "Our family is now a family of faith. I want others to have that same experience of knowing God."

Many other families are discovering the love of Jesus through the ministry of Little Lambs. Rick and Maryann brought their children to Little Lambs, experienced the love of God, and began attending the church. They are now members. Rose Ann and her children were enfolded by Coffee Break and Little Lambs and have seen lots of wonderful changes in their family life. Rose Ann says, "My children and I learned about patient, persistent prayer through Coffee Break and Little Lambs. We prayed for my husband for seven years, and the Lord heard our prayers. I believe that God used the crafts and materials from Little Lambs to soften my husband's heart." Healing for the heart—it's what we all need.

Prayer

Dear Jesus, thank you for loving me and for living in my heart. Help me to share your love and bring hope and healing to all I meet, young or old. Amen.

A New Self

You were taught, with regard to your former way of life, to put off your old self, which is being corrupted by its deceitful desires; to be made new in the attitude of your minds; and to put on the new self, created to be like God in true righteousness and holiness.

—Ephesians 4:22-23

The soft voice on the other end of the phone had a lilting accent. I closed my eyes to better concentrate on our conversation and tried to imagine what Young-Kyo Kim looked like. I pictured a beautiful Korean woman with dark hair, dark eyes, and a sensitive soul. I could only imagine her hair and eye color, but her responses to my questions gave me a window into her soul. Young-Kyo was eager to tell her story. "I want to share how Coffee Break has touched my heart," she said. "I want to let others know how the power of God's Word made me a new person. Where shall I begin?"

Young was born and raised in Korea. She graduated from Ewha Women's University before coming to the United States to study at Columbia University. Her education had provided her with an excellent academic foundation for life. But in spite of a good career, a happy marriage, and motherhood, she felt that something was missing from her life. "I didn't know what it was," she said, "but I was never satisfied. There was always an emptiness. I tried to fill it with many things, but nothing took away the longing inside." Young's need to be fulfilled led her to push herself toward perfection. "I tried to be a good wife, good mother, good daughter-in-law, good neighbor, good sister, good deacon. But I had only twenty-four hours a day to be good, and I felt I could never be good enough."

Then came the day a routine physical check-up was no longer routine, and Young was diagnosed with cancer. Suddenly she had an opportunity to look at "the good life" from a new perspective. Being perfect was no longer important to her. "I knew I had to change my lifestyle," she said. "Having cancer provided me with an opportunity to slow down and reevaluate my priorities." It also provided Young with the opportunity to use her gifts as a poet; she wrote a bilingual book of poetry reflecting on her life's journey. The opening verses of her poem "Chemo Hair" express her thoughts during that time:

So pathetic is the scene of my hair-picking mornings.
The sheet and pillow case are the white background for the haired flower design.
But, I am thankful because I am becoming an expert hair
hunter as each morning goes by.

One clump, two clumps. I pore over the cadavers of my hair.
But, I am thankful because the hair on my head outnumbers the cadavers.

Three clumps, four clumps. I am struck by the lackluster,
inelastic youth of my life.
But, I am thankful for the rest of my life yet to come.

Clumps of hair are the colors of my pain.
But, I am thankful because I still have the head left, on which to grow a forest of hair.

—from *Traffic Lights* (Seoul, Korea: HyeHwaDang, 1998)

After the chemotherapy treatment had ended, a friend invited Young to Coffee Break. Her first visit was at the end of the season, in late April. In spite of the warmth of the spring morning she came to the group wearing a red knit hat. That day the group shared what God had done in their lives through their year of study and discussion. Young was moved by the openness of the sharing, and when the group was ready to dismiss, she said, "I want to share too." She took off her red hat, revealing her bald head, the result of the chemotherapy. Her gesture of openness was symbolic of her willingness to be open to the process of change in her life.

That day marked a turning point in Young's life. She began to faithfully attend Coffee Break, and the Word touched her heart. Gradually the emptiness she had experienced was replaced with a new understanding of God's presence in her life. "Before coming to Coffee Break the Bible was a textbook that I believed with my head but not with my heart," she said. "I realized Coffee Break had a different approach, and I found what I had been looking for all these years." The opportunity to discover the Bible in a small group setting was the bridge to Young's personal relationship with God. By the time the group had completed the next study guide, Young had experienced a double blessing. She had fullness of joy, and she had a full head of beautiful black hair. The cancer was gone. She was healed in body and in soul.

Young used her experiences with cancer and with Coffee Break studies to examine her life and to draw closer to God, expressing her thoughts in the conclusion of her poem:

> The habit of throwing away one strand and
> two strands of filthy-looking hair
> taught me to rid myself of greed.
> I am thankful because I have now become busy searching
> for the strands of sin in my heart.
>
> The fallen hair is darkness.
> Newly sprouted hair is light.
> Despair is the fallen hair.
> Hope is the new sprouts about to come.
> I am thankful for the river of yesteryear that has carried
> away all darkness and despair.
>
> Thankfulness seeps into my empty head, empty heart, and empty hands
> as the light and hope stride quietly into my life.
> What blessing can be greater than this?
> Tears of thankfulness support my bowed head.

Looking back, Young is grateful for what she has learned through cancer and through Coffee Break. Together they opened the door to a new self. "In time I accepted cancer as a gift," she said. "It taught me that I needed to make changes in my life. But it was in Coffee Break that I met the Lord. As I studied God's Word, I realized that I needed to 'put off' my selfishness and greed. I had to 'put on' a new self. Today my heart is filled with the Lord, and I want to turn my suffering into service." Young's poetry is an expression of that desire to serve.

Sometimes, as Young discovered, a crisis in our lives becomes a spiritual turning point. A life-threatening illness brought about the death of Young's old way of life and ushered in a new attitude focused on Christ. That same newness is available to each of us. We don't need to experience a crisis to start the soul-searching process. As you reflect on Young's poem, ask yourself, What strands of sin do I need to throw away? Pride? A bad habit? A critical nature? An unforgiving spirit? Let the Holy Spirit do the chemotherapy in your heart, and then put on the new self, "created to be like God in true righteousness and holiness."

Prayer

Create in me a clean heart, O God, and renew a right spirit within me. Amen.

Like a Child

At that time the disciples came to Jesus and asked, "Who is the greatest in the kingdom of heaven?" Jesus called a little child and had him stand among them. And he said: "I tell you the truth, unless you change and become like little children, you will never enter the kingdom of heaven. Therefore, whoever humbles himself like this child is the greatest in the kingdom of heaven. And whoever welcomes a little child like this in my name welcomes me."

—Matthew 18:1-5

Carol picked up the crying infant in the Coffee Break nursery, settled into the rocking chair, and softly began to sing a song she remembered from her Sunday school days.

> Jesus loves me, this I know,
> for the Bible tells me so.
> Little ones to him belong;
> they are weak, but he is strong.
> Yes, Jesus loves me! Yes, Jesus loves me!
> Yes, Jesus loves me! The Bible tells me so.

As Carol continued her gentle rocking and humming, the little one gradually quieted down. Somehow this song never failed to provide the needed comfort. Jesus really does love these little children, Carol quietly reflected as she cuddled the child in her arms.

Caring for the children in the nursery reminded Carol of the happiness of her own early childhood. "When I was a little girl I thought I had the perfect family," Carol said. "I loved my mom and dad and our home. I didn't want a thing to change." But Carol's parents divorced when she was an adolescent, and her secure world changed in an instant. "I felt lost without my father, and I missed my older siblings," she recalled. "Somehow I thought it was my fault that our family was no longer together, and I carried that guilt inside me for many years." Carol's teen years were difficult. Her mother remarried, and Carol was abused by her stepfather. "Those experiences were painful," she said softly. "I was certain God had abandoned me, and I tried to cover up my pain by hiding from people and from God."

Carol withdrew, avoiding people as much as she could. In time she was diagnosed with agoraphobia, a strong fear of being in an open space. "I didn't even know what that meant," she said, "but I had the disease, all right. I seldom left my home, and I was afraid of everything and everybody, including God. I was very lonely and just wanted to die." To help her overcome her difficulties, Carol sought help from a Christian counselor, who eventually introduced her to the coordinator of the local Coffee Break program. It didn't take long for this coordinator to recognize Carol's love for children, and she invited Carol to be one of the nursery attendants for the weekly Coffee Break Bible study. Carol was willing to help with child care, but it took her three attempts before she was able to enter the unfamiliar territory of the church. Encouraged by the smiling face of the director and the warm welcome of the other helpers, Carol soon felt the nursery to be a safe haven.

Carol looked forward to Wednesday mornings. She and her husband had no children of their own, and taking care of the children for their appreciative mothers was rewarding. As Carol spent time reading to the infants and toddlers and singing "Jesus Loves Me" to them, she began to realize God's love. "You can't sing or talk about Jesus' love for children without that love rubbing off a little on you. God was using these precious little ones to lead me to him. Could it be possible God even cared about me? Did God know my pain? Did God see the scars that I had tried so desperately to hide from the outside world for so many years?"

So Carol's faith journey was renewed in the nursery as she cared for God's little ones. This renewal continued when she was invited to a summer session of evening Coffee Break, where she remembers being "a quiet participant, but a very good listener." Carol came to those sessions with a child's eagerness to learn. Caring for children had softened her heart, enabling her to be receptive, but the truth of God's love for her needed to come through the study of God's Word. "It was only a six-week summer session, but I learned so much," Carol said. "I learned that I didn't have to be perfect to be loved by God. That was like a weight rolling off my shoulders. I discovered that I didn't need to earn my own salvation; Jesus paid it all when he died for my sins." That message started to sink in. Carol was learning that the kingdom of heaven was for people like herself who come to God in childlike faith.

That summer was a turning point in Carol's life; she could see that the healing was underway. No longer fearful, no longer withdrawn, she began to see the world with different eyes. "I saw the blossoming trees, the beautiful flowers, and I even heard the birds singing," said Carol. One day she noticed a row of cherry trees in bloom. "Had they been there all the time? It was the first time I had actually *seen* them," she recalled. "Experiencing God's love had opened my eyes. I was happier than I had been in years. And it all began in the nursery. I thought the children needed me, but it was I who needed the nursery."

When the Story Hour program needed a helper, Carol was asked to fill that role. There her faith grew even more. Preparing and listening to the stories week after week was like being bathed in God's love and care—the teachers grew right along with the children. For Carol, one of the best parts of Story Hour was watching the children's joy when they got to take home the special teddy bear called the Prayer Bear as a reminder to pray that week. Carol loved teddy bears, and she often thought, "Wouldn't it be fun to be a child again and be the one to take the Prayer Bear home?"

During this time of healing, Carol and her husband decided to attend church. As she put it, "It was time to quit running away from God and run to him." The spiritual growth that began in the nursery rocking chair continued to be nurtured in the church pew and through fellowship with other believers. Nine years after Carol first volunteered in the nursery, she and her husband professed their faith in Jesus Christ and joined the church where she had discovered that Jesus loved her too. The Coffee Break women provided music for that joyful service, and the Story Hour leaders gave Carol her very own Prayer Bear—to keep forever.

The next time you sing "Jesus Loves Me"—whether it's in the nursery, in Little Lambs or Story Hour, or with your own children or grandchildren—try singing the song to yourself as well as to the children in your care. As you sing, let the full meaning of the words sink deep into your heart and soul. "Yes, *Jesus* loves me! Yes, Jesus *loves* me! Yes, Jesus loves *me*! The Bible tells me so." Then remind yourself of the words of John 1:12: "To all who received him, to those who believed in his name, he gave the right to become children of God." You are—and forever shall remain—a child of God.

Prayer

Father God, help me to come to you in childlike faith. Precious Jesus, thank you for loving even me. Holy Spirit, keep my spirit humbly receptive. Lord, I come. Amen.

Walking in the Light

God is light; in him there is no darkness at all. If we claim to have fellowship with him yet walk in the darkness, we lie and do not live by the truth. But if we walk in the light, as he is in the light, we have fellowship with one another, and the blood of Jesus, his Son, purifies us from all sin.

—1 John 1:5-7

It was summer, the season of Little League baseball. Alejandra spent lots of time at the park watching her son play ball. She usually sat along the sidelines with the other mothers, enjoying casual conversation as the game progressed. That's how Alejandra met Vicky. Their sons were on the same team, and they saw each other at every game. Alejandra had lived in California since she was three, when her family moved from Mexico. But she was new to this community and was eager for friendship. So when Vicky told her about a program at Vicky's church, Alejandra welcomed the opportunity to attend.

"Vicky was so nice, so friendly," Alejandra remembered. "I needed friends, and I looked forward to going to her Bible study." When the baseball season ended, Alejandra watched the mail for the promised invitation, and in the fall, she began to attend Sobremesa, a Spanish-language variation of Coffee Break. There she found the friendship she had been looking for. But she also discovered much more.

Sobremesa reflects a commitment to minister to the diversity within God's family. The materials are written in Spanish and are structured to reach men and women for whom a personal Bible study might be a new experience. The small group discussions are focused on the Bible, conducted in Spanish, and led by men or women from within the Latino community. A relatively new approach for Coffee Break, Sobremesa is reaching men and women with the gospel and providing for spiritual needs, as Alejandra can testify.

Alejandra had not been in a church for years when she showed up for the first small group session. As she reflected on those first Sobremesa meetings she recalled, "Bible study was new to me, but everyone was so kind and so helpful. I liked it, and I wanted to keep coming." The love and acceptance in the small group contrasted sharply with Alejandra's past experiences. "Before coming to Sobremesa my life had been full of disappointment and pain," she confided. "At sixteen I ran away from home to be with my boyfriend. When I became pregnant and the relationship became abusive, I had no choice but to go back home to my parents."

After her son was born Alejandra's problems intensified. "My life was difficult, and I was very, very unhappy," she remembered. In time she became so disillusioned that she attempted suicide. She was nineteen years old. "I hated myself, and I hated my life so much that I wanted to die." she said. But God had another plan for Alejandra, and she did not die. She remembered, "I woke up in the hospital and was returned to my family's home. I was angry with my situation, angry with who I was, and I was miserable."

Eventually Alejandra found a job and an apartment and was able to care for her small son on her own. When she committed to a new relationship and had two more children, she attempted to put the pieces of her life back together. But the sense of darkness from the past continued to cloud the present. "The wrong choices I made as a young person affected my life, and there were problems. I'd get angry with my kids or angry with myself," she reflected. "It was hard for me to accept who I was." As Alejandra continued with Sobremesa, she began to see qualities in the leaders and members of the small group that she wanted in her own life. She admired and respected the women who were her new friends, and she wanted her life to be filled with the joy she saw in them.

Alejandra discovered that reading and discussing the Bible in a small group is an excellent way to discover how to walk in the light of God's love. She learned new things every week. One day her group discussed the topic "giving your life to Christ." Intrigued, she wondered, "How does that happen? Do I say something? Do I feel something?" She tucked her thoughts away in her heart, and even though she didn't know when she would do this, she knew that having a relationship with God through Jesus was something she wanted for herself.

A couple of weeks later her Sobremesa leader, Sonia, presented a lesson on accepting Christ, using a pamphlet called *The Bridge to New Life*. As Sonia talked about the great gap that separates sinful people from a holy God, Alejandra began to cry. Then Sonia went on to explain how Jesus Christ is the "bridge" between humanity and God. Alejandra realized this was the moment she had been anticipating. "I felt something inside of me," she related. "Something was telling me to say, 'Yes, I want to accept Christ.'" When Sonia asked Alejandra, "Why are you crying?" Alejandra replied, "I don't want to be separated from God." Then Sonia led Alejandra in a prayer of repentance and faith that brought her from darkness to light.

Since that day Alejandra's life has changed for the better. "I still have problems," she said, "but every time I have a problem I open the Bible and I find what I need." Alejandra has discovered that the Bible brings comfort, and it is a guide for life. "I don't know how it happens, but when I open the Bible, I am always on the right page." Alejandra has noticed other changes in her life as well. She is less angry with herself and with her children, and she is working hard to change some old habits. "I cleaned up my language," she said. "No more swearing. I know my children follow my example." Alejandra and her family are active in their church, and their faith is growing stronger every day. "My whole world changed after I came to Sobremesa," Alejandra related. "I am so much happier. I don't know how to say it, I am . . . blessed? Yes, that's the word. I am blessed."

Today Alejandra has a strong desire to witness to her new walk with the Lord. She wrote the following testimony for Sobremesa:

¡Sobremesa me ha llenado de entusiasmo! Gracias al grupo pequeño al que asisto pude encontrar lo que tanto necesitaba: compañerismo, amistad, amor y lo más importante, a Cristo. Ahora mi vida ha cambiado. Doy gracias a Dios por ponerme allí.

Sobremesa has filled me with enthusiasm! Thanks to the small group I participate in, I was able to find what I so desperately needed: companionship, friendship, love, and most importantly I found Christ. Now my life has changed. I give thanks to God for placing me in my small group.

Alejandra now walks in the light of God's love because two women walked alongside her in friendship and in love, offering an invitation to a small group and an invitation to know Jesus. Ask God to give you the courage to follow their example today.

Prayer

Dear Lord Jesus, thank you for being the light of the world. Help me to walk in your light and to share your love with someone today. Amen.

Teach Me Your Paths

To you, O Lord, I lift up my soul;

in you I trust, O my God.

Show me your ways, O Lord,

teach me your paths;

guide me in your truth and teach me,

for you are God my Savior,

and my hope is in you all day long.

—Psalm 25:1, 4-5

Alice put her toddler into the stroller and helped her kindergartner, Jacob, zip up his jacket. Then the three of them walked the familiar path between home and school. Twice a day this activity was part of Alice's routine, and she enjoyed it. In addition to being important for Jacob, the stroller ride kept her younger daughter contented, and Alice got to meet Jacob's friends and their moms. Taking good care of her family was important to Alice. She took pride in her ability to keep things running smoothly. The walk to school was just another part of her organized day.

Alice's family was the center of her focus, and she poured her energy into meeting their needs. This was a big commitment, for Jacob had been diagnosed with cerebral palsy at birth. Caring for him was a time-consuming and sometimes draining responsibility. Jacob's initial prognosis had been grim. "The specialists never expected him to walk, talk, or be 'self-tending,'" Alice explained. However, Jacob had surpassed everyone's expectations and was now in kindergarten.

Much of the children's daily care fell on Alice's shoulders. "My husband's executive position required him to be away from home as many as twenty days each month, and my second child was a very active toddler," she said. "But I considered myself responsible, self-sufficient, confident, and resourceful." As Alice walked the busy path of her life she believed she was headed in the right direction.

One day, as Alice and Jacob were walking home from school, they were joined by Jacob's classmate Eddie and his mother, Debbie. Jacob and Eddie seemed to have a special bond. When Alice commented on this, Debbie explained that her sister had cerebral palsy, and Eddie was familiar with the challenges presented by that condition. Alice welcomed Debbie's friendship. When Debbie told her about a Bible study she had recently joined, Alice was interested. "Coffee Break sounded good to me," Alice remembered.

"My motivation to attend was purely selfish in the beginning. I needed to do something for myself, and this was as good as anything." In response to Debbie's invitation Alice started down the path of Scripture study that would give her life a brand-new direction.

Like many women who attend Coffee Break small groups, Alice had been raised in a Christian environment. "I had been given Bible knowledge as I was growing up, but as an adult I made Scripture suit my needs," she said. "I had a customized approach to what I believed the Bible said, and I took what I wanted." The church attendance that had been part of Alice's childhood was pushed into the background by a busy family schedule. Alice realized that the spiritual side of her life was slowly being depleted. "Caring for a special-needs child is an exhausting experience," she said. "If you don't have a lot in your spiritual bank, you go bankrupt very quickly." The weekly opportunity for Bible study in the context of friendship and fellowship had a lot of appeal. "Coffee, cookies, encouragement and love, plus Little Lambs for my toddler—I loved it," she said with a smile. "Wednesdays became my Sundays." As Alice began her Coffee Break journey, she had no idea that the pathway would be so rewarding and the discoveries so life-changing.

Week after week Alice attended Coffee Break, and week after week she moved forward in her spiritual journey. "It wasn't always easy to get to the meetings," she remembered. "There were a lot of obstacles in my path, but I didn't want to give up." The continuing weekly Bible study gradually made an impact on Alice's spiritual life, and she realized that her perspectives were taking a new direction. The Holy Spirit used sustained contact with God's Word to reveal new truths to her, truths that were at times difficult to accept. "I struggled to absorb what I was discovering," she confessed. "Our group was studying the gospel of Luke, and Jesus' teachings were very clear about life and faith. My faith—my belief system—was not based on God's truth." The Holy Spirit had put Alice on the path of faith, and as the truth flowed from Scripture to her heart and mind, she knew she needed to make some changes in her life's direction.

Coffee Break leaders will agree that the study of God's Word is a powerful instrument of change. Week after week and year after year, leaders have the privilege of observing the Holy Spirit at work as their groups study the Scriptures. "As I continued with the studies," said Alice, "Coffee Break opened up new ideas for me. The meetings became more than my peaceful island in the week, and I discovered challenges I couldn't ignore." The gospel message the group discussed not only pointed to the way of salvation, it also showed the need for surrender. "I knew about salvation," Alice related, "but I never knew what it meant for Jesus to be Lord of my life. Asking God to take control was a new thought for me. It meant I'd have to change." As the Holy Spirit continued to guide her thoughts, Alice knew she needed to decide who was in charge. "I decided I wanted God to be the master of my heart and the central focus in my life," she said. The surrender came during a time of personal, private prayer, as she asked God to forgive her sins and give her a heart that followed his leading.

God is faithful. As Alice followed, God led her from coast to coast and from learner to leader. Today Alice directs the Coffee Break ministry in her church. "I remember my early years of Coffee Break," she commented. "I have a lot of compassion for young moms who face demanding schedules and challenging lives." But Alice also has a passion for what God continues to teach her, for involvement in Coffee Break opens up new dimensions to God's will every day.

Alice knows that Coffee Break offers friendship and fellowship, but so much more besides. It offers the opportunity to walk with God on a daily basis. "Through Coffee Break I discovered the excitement of following where God was leading me," she said with conviction. "Now I am eager to help others discover the path God has prepared." For Alice walking with the Lord is an ongoing process that begins with one step.

That first step may lead you to surrender, to share Christ, or to lead others. But wherever your path leads, you don't need to walk alone. God has promised to guide your steps.

Prayer

To you, O Lord, I lift up my soul; in you I trust, O my God. Show me your ways, O Lord, teach me your paths; guide me in your truth and teach me, for you are God my Savior, and my hope is in you all day long. Amen.

Chosen by the Father

For we know, brothers and sisters beloved by God, that he has chosen you, because our message of the gospel came to you not in word only, but also in power and in the Holy Spirit and with full conviction. . . . For in spite of persecution you received the word with joy inspired by the Holy Spirit.

—1 Thessalonians 1:4-6 (NRSV)

Eight-year-old Maria closed her eyes to shut out the shadowy images in her darkening bedroom and silently began to recite a prayer the nuns had taught her: "Our Father who art in heaven, hallowed be thy name." Praying the Lord's Prayer had become a nightly pattern, and the familiar words brought a sense of peace and comfort into Maria's otherwise confusing and difficult life. Maria's family had left their home in Argentina to escape the fear of revolution in that country, but for little Maria adjusting to life in the United States was not easy. "I did not speak or understand English, and we moved almost every year while my father searched for work or went to school. Changing schools so often was difficult, and we didn't always find acceptance in our new neighborhoods."

Maria's parents were not religious, but they did send their children to Catholic catechism and church for a brief time "so we would fit into American society better." Maria remembers walking to Mass with her brothers and sister on Sunday mornings. "My parents never came with us," she said. "And even though I didn't understand a word that anyone was saying, I loved being in church. I felt safe there." For Maria it was a comfort to think of God as a father, and it was in catechism that she learned to pray the Lord's Prayer.

Most believers know the Lord's Prayer by heart. Do you remember learning it as a child? Who taught you to pray? Perhaps, like mine, your experience was "at your mother's knee." But many women and children in Coffee Break and Story Hour have a different story of coming to faith. Maria's is one of those stories.

While it is true that Maria's parents sent her to catechism, they also warned her not to be brainwashed by the religious teaching she would receive there. "My parents did not believe in God, and they did everything they could to convince me that God did not exist." Maria remembers a big fat Bible her mother had purchased to record the family tree. It sat on the bookshelf in their suburban ranch home and Maria was curious about it. "I had been in school long enough to read English," she said, "and one day I began to read this Bible. I was amazed at what I read." Maria's amazement led her to question her mother about the Bible. "When I asked my mother questions about it she became very angry and told me to stop. She said the Bible was a novel that could have been written by any number of people while they were sitting around a campfire. She told me that religion was only for weak people who couldn't think for themselves."

These were discouraging words for a ten-year-old, and from then on Maria decided to keep her religious questions to herself. In her own mind she refused to believe her mother's words, and while she did not know exactly who God was, she knew her prayers to him were real. In her young heart she chose to believe that God cared for her.

Throughout her years of schooling Maria continued to pray and to believe in God as "our Father in heaven." Her desire to know more about this heavenly Father eventually led her to enroll in a Catholic college, where she was given a textbook understanding of Christianity. Her parents refused to support her either emotionally or financially and believed she was making a foolish choice. Still she held on to her private prayers and to the nugget of truth that God was real. And God, who *is* real and knows our hearts, led Maria to meet and marry a Christian man. Maria began to see that God was working in her life. A foundation of faith was being laid on which she could continue to build.

As a young married woman Maria tried to study the Bible but was never successful in seeing its relevance for her personal life. God remained for her a distant figure, and Maria often felt unworthy of the blessings she was experiencing. Then, after moving to a new community, Maria was invited to Coffee Break. "From the first meeting I knew this was what I had been seeking all these years. The personal approach gave me a hunger to discover what the Bible could say to my life. I was amazed that the Bible was speaking directly to me. It wasn't just a history book anymore, but a personal letter from my heavenly Father." In the small group setting Maria's faith began to grow and blossom. She discovered the joy of praying with and being prayed for by the members of her group. In time she agreed to serve as a coleader of a group. The fearful little girl from Argentina who had found comfort in reciting the Lord's Prayer was discovering the "message of the gospel in power and with full conviction."

It was Maria's turn to lead the lesson in the study of Paul's letter to the Thessalonians. As she was preparing the lesson material, she had what she later called "one crystallizing moment"—a moment that enabled her to see herself as "beloved by God," as one "chosen" by the Father. A moment that erased the years of unanswered spiritual questions, that compensated for any lack of religious heritage. A moment that blotted out any shame or scorn she had experienced in her search to know God. The apostle Paul became the spiritual father she longed for, as he wrote words that guided, consoled, reassured his readers who "in spite of persecution . . . received the word with joy." "Paul was writing about me—this was my story," she said. And Maria experienced a marvelous moment of grace.

As the study of Paul's letters to the Thessalonians continued, Maria began to share her life story with her group. "I never realized I could share my spiritual history with others. I had kept my prayer life and my search for God hidden within myself for so many years because of my mother's strong feelings against God. I often felt ashamed of my poor religious background, and I didn't think my story was significant. Because of Coffee Break, I came to see that I have a story to tell. It's a story of God's grace, important only because it shows how God drew me and chose me to be God's child since the day I was born. It is grace and grace alone that makes a person worthy."

Have you told your story of God's grace? Take some time today to reflect on the truth that God has "chosen you"; you are "beloved by God." Find a friend and share your joy in knowing that you have been chosen by the Father to receive the gospel.

Prayer

Father God, thank you for loving me and choosing me to belong to you. Give me the grace to be a story sharer today. Amen.

The Good News About Jesus

An angel of the Lord said to Philip, "Go south to the road—the desert road—that goes down from Jerusalem to Gaza." So he started out, and on his way he met an Ethiopian . . . [who] was sitting in his chariot reading the book of Isaiah the prophet. . . .

Philip ran up to the chariot and heard the man reading Isaiah the prophet. "Do you understand what you are reading?" Philip asked.

"How can I," he said, "unless someone explains it to me?" So he invited Philip to come up and sit with him. . . .

Then Philip began with that very passage of Scripture and told him the good news about Jesus.

—Acts 8:26-31, 35

"There I was, sitting at my kitchen table, trying to make sense of this Bible passage. I wasn't on a desert road and I wasn't in a chariot, but that Ethiopian and I had something in common—neither of us understood what we were reading. I was ready to give up on this Coffee Break thing." With no church background and no previous Bible study experience, Stephanie was feeling pretty lost. How could she understand unless someone explained it to her? When she told her neighbor, Dawn, that she was quitting the Bible study, Dawn replied that she wasn't giving up on Stephanie, and she offered to travel this road with her for as long as it took. Dawn became the Philip in Stephanie's story. Stephanie's kitchen table became a chariot, and, as Stephanie put it, "I was off for the ride of my life!"

Stephanie was excited as she shared her story. She had met Dawn through an ad in the Bargain Corner of the local paper. Stephanie and her family were preparing for a move, and they had some furniture to sell. Dawn was buying, and the two got acquainted. "It turned out we were moving to Dawn's neighborhood, and I guess that's when she began praying about asking me to Coffee Break. I needed the prayers all right. My husband and I were experiencing financial difficulties, our marriage was in trouble, and my mother was ill with a terminal disease. I was feeling so lost with no hope for the future. My two little children were all that kept me from throwing in the towel."

Stephanie accepted Dawn's invitation to Coffee Break in the fall. The group was studying the book of Jonah. "I was willing to give it a try," Stephanie recalled, "but it was a struggle for me to understand the lesson material. I know how the Ethiopian felt as he was reading the prophet Isaiah, because that's how I felt as I was reading the prophet Jonah—completely overwhelmed. That's when I decided to quit, and that's when Dawn climbed into my chariot, which really was my kitchen table."

The two women met to study the Bible together one night a week for several weeks that fall. Stephanie had many questions, but Dawn was patient and never judgmental. Stephanie remembered, "I was discovering things about God and Jesus that I had never imagined. As a child I hadn't gone to church. I had no spiritual history and no idea how a person became a Christian. The idea of the Holy Spirit was a real revelation, for while I believed that God was out there somewhere, I never made the connection that he could be in here—in me."

One night, after the two had studied together for several weeks, Dawn asked Stephanie if she wanted Jesus to be Lord of her life. "This was a brand-new idea to me. I told Dawn, 'You'll have to tell me what to do.' Together we bowed our heads in prayer, and right there at my kitchen table I prayed the prayer of repentance and accepted Jesus as my Lord and Savior. God gave me an incredible sense of peace and of his presence. For the first time in a long time I believed that there was hope for me—hope for my family—hope for the future."

Dawn continued to disciple Stephanie, and their Coffee Break leaders kept on praying for them both. "I'd love to tell you that from that day on life was a bed of roses, but that would not be true," Stephanie said. "I had a long way to go in order to fully accept that God loved me and wanted me in his forever family. Growing up I felt rejected by my father because I was an unplanned child, an 'accident.' I felt that my life was a mistake and that I was responsible for my parents' unhappy marriage. Dawn helped me realize that God loved me and intended that I would be born. There was a plan and a purpose for my life. As I continued to read and study the Bible my faith grew stronger. I still remember the day when I discovered the Scripture that told me how God cares for the birds of the air and the lilies of the field. 'If God cares about a flower,' I thought, 'then he must care about me.'"

Coffee Break became an important part of Stephanie's life. Her family began to worship together, and in time they joined the church. The leaders provided support during the final days of her mother's illness, encouraging Stephanie to share her faith with her mother before she died. It was during this time that Stephanie learned about the prayers of the leaders for her and her family. One of the leaders kept a prayer journal and had written as an entry on November 1, 1994, "Stephanie accepted the Lord today." "I was amazed to learn of their prayers," she said. "A group of women who barely knew me cared enough to pray for me and my family all those months. I am so grateful."

Gratitude has prompted Stephanie to prepare for a leadership role in Coffee Break with the goal of reaching the lost for Christ. "I can't imagine where I'd be today if Dawn hadn't invited me to Coffee Break and told me the good news about Jesus. Not only has it changed my life, it has changed my family's history. The chorus from the song 'Thank You' by Ray Boltz expresses my feelings so well."

Thank you for giving to the Lord, for I am a life that
   was changed.
Thank you for giving to the Lord. I am so glad you
   gave.

— © 1988 Gaither Music Company ASCAP.
All rights reserved. Used by permission.

Stephanie's testimony is an encouragement to all of us to continue praying for our unchurched neighbors. All around us are women who are well-groomed and beautiful on the outside but lost and hopeless within. They are waiting for an invitation to Coffee Break. They are waiting for a Philip to tell them the good news about Jesus. Could that Philip be you? You don't need a chariot; a kitchen table will do just fine. Pray for an opportunity today.

Prayer

Dear Jesus, I do want to be a witness for you. I confess my fears and pray for the Holy Spirit's power and courage to be the one to tell the good news to another, and then to another, and another. Amen.

Rest for the Weary

Come to me, all you who are weary and burdened, and I will give you rest. Take my yoke upon you and learn from me, for I am gentle and humble in heart, and you will find rest for your souls. For my yoke is easy and my burden is light.

—Matthew 11:28-30

The loud crying of an infant woke DeeEtta from a sound sleep. It took a moment before she realized it was *her* baby who was crying. Motherhood is a lot of work, she thought as she picked up her newborn. Will this baby ever sleep through the night? He sure cries a lot. The baby quieted down as DeeEtta fed him. In spite of the interrupted sleep this was always a special time for the two of them. When baby Travis was feeding, he was content, and DeeEtta had time to think about her life.

During those middle-of-the-night feedings, DeeEtta often thought back to the time, months earlier, when she discovered that she was pregnant. "I made a lot of bad choices during my high school years," she recalled. "But after high school I was ready to go straight. I broke up with my boyfriend, and then two weeks later found out I was pregnant." DeeEtta didn't know how she would manage, but she knew she wanted to keep her baby. "Lots of my friends had abortions, but I didn't want to go that route," she said. Instead, DeeEtta looked in the Yellow Pages under the heading "Family Doctor" and made an appointment to be examined.

At the doctor's office DeeEtta filled out the necessary forms and was examined. She was told, "Yes, you are pregnant." That she expected. But the actions that followed caught her by surprise. "I was in an examining room, and my clothes were in another room, so I couldn't leave. A nurse showed me a video and offered me a *free* abortion. It would have been so easy to go through with it. No one else knew." But God knew and DeeEtta knew, and while she had little to do with God in those days, she said no to the abortion and asked for her clothes.

When Travis was born, DeeEtta faced the challenges of raising her son as a single mother. "I was nineteen years old. I had no job. I had no car. I had no husband," she said. "I was trying to be the perfect parent, and I was doing it alone. It was exhausting." Being a parent is hard work. Being a single parent is even harder, as DeeEtta discovered.

"My mom was supportive, but I was on my own, and it wasn't easy."

About the same time that DeeEtta gave birth to Travis, a church in the Pacific Northwest where DeeEtta lived was planning to start a Coffee Break Bible study. One of the leaders put her own baby in a stroller and walked the neighborhood, knocking on doors and inviting women and children to attend the Bible study and Story Hour. The flyer she handed out listed a free nursery for infants, and DeeEtta decided to give it a try. She liked it. "It was wonderful to put Travis in the nursery one morning a week," DeeEtta said. "I don't remember what we studied that spring, but I do remember how relieved I felt each Wednesday as I handed my baby to the nursery staff. It was just the break I needed."

The Coffee Break leaders provided DeeEtta with more than a break. They became the models and mentors she needed as she made a life for herself and her little son. Week after week DeeEtta looked, listened, and learned from God's Word and from the staff of Coffee Break, Story Hour, and the nursery. "The leaders and workers were wonderful," she remembered. "The nursery workers stopped by my home to see how I was doing during the week, and my leader often invited me to her home to share lunch with her after Coffee Break. The fact that they cared about me made me feel good, but it also made my burden as a single mom much lighter." DeeEtta was seeing God's love through the love the leaders poured out on her.

DeeEtta continued attending Coffee Break for the next two years. Travis moved from nursery to the Story Hour room for two-year-olds as his mom moved forward in her understanding of God. "I enjoyed what I was learning about God and about life," she said. "Every time I had a question I could go to the leaders. They never made me feel foolish." Soon DeeEtta was attending church on Sundays, where she discovered as warm a welcome as she had found on Wednesdays. "The friendship and encouragement from people at church meant a lot to me," she remembered. "I watched how my new friends cared for their children and interacted with their husbands. I saw firsthand how Christian families treated each other, and I wanted the same kind of life for myself."

One morning after Coffee Break DeeEtta went to pick up her child in the Story Hour room. Her leader, Donna, also stopped at the room, and the two women began talking as Travis continued playing with the toys. "We were sitting on the floor," DeeEtta remembered. "Suddenly I realized that everyone else was gone, and the three of us were alone in the room." The two women talked about Coffee Break, the Bible, and life in general. Then Donna, sensing that the time was right, asked DeeEtta, "Do you want to accept Jesus as your Savior?" DeeEtta was ready—she gladly said yes.

Together the two prayed a prayer of repentance and faith right there on the Story Hour rug. "I was so happy," DeeEtta recalled. "I wanted to run and jump and shout. I felt like I was floating in the air. I was filled with a desire to tell others of my experience and my faith."

DeeEtta's desire to share her experience and to grow in her faith kept her active and involved in both Coffee Break and church. She brought her new boyfriend to church, where he was befriended and discipled. He also became a Christian. And when DeeEtta decided to marry him, the Coffee Break women helped plan her wedding. The women who had shared DeeEtta's burdens now shared her joy.

DeeEtta and her husband became involved in the activities of the church, first as attenders and then as leaders. DeeEtta worked in Story Hour and led Coffee Break. "Gratitude is my motivation," she said. "So many women carried my burden when I was in need. Now I can give back to God and the church."

Both shared burdens and shared joys are part of the Coffee Break experience as leaders reach out in friendship. The free nursery drew DeeEtta to Coffee Break, but the friendship kept her coming. She was weary and needed physical rest as much as spiritual rest. One-another evangelism involves both physical relationships and spiritual teachings. It means that we carry each other's burdens as we lead others to the one who has carried our burden.

Prayer

Lord, thank you for the invitation to come to you with my burden. Give me the strength and desire to share the burdens of others, knowing that you will give the rest that each of us needs. Amen.

Lord, Hear My Cry

Glorify the LORD *with me;*

let us exalt his name together.

I sought the LORD*, and he answered me;*

he delivered me from all my fears.

Those who look to him are radiant;

their faces are never covered with shame.

The righteous cry out, and the LORD *hears them;*

he delivers them from all their troubles.

—Psalm 34:3-5, 17

It was Easter Sunday and Jackie and her husband had spent the day visiting with family. It had been a good day with plenty of food, laughter, and conversation. "My husband wanted to stay longer," Jackie recalled, "but something told me we needed to get home." Jackie's intuition was right, for when they arrived home they received a message that her father had died that day. "I felt a flood of emotions," she said. "I was twenty-five years old, pregnant with my first child, and not prepared to lose my father."

Jackie's husband went to bed, but Jackie couldn't sleep. She went out on the front porch and sat on the steps. "I was crying and praying all at the same time," she recalled. As Jackie looked up into the night sky she saw the stars sparkling overhead. She called out to God, "Lord, are you really there? I need you now. Help me to find you—to see you in someone or something." Jackie had been searching for a meaningful relationship with God for a long time. Her heart told her that God was the only one who could bring the comfort she needed, and in her grief she cried out to him. God heard her prayer. Even though Jackie couldn't see it then, God had a plan to provide for her deepest needs.

Jackie's search for a relationship with God had begun when she was a young girl of twelve or thirteen. "I went to summer camp that year," she recalled. "Camp Tall Turf was a great experience, and there I gave my life to Christ." But when she came home from camp, she didn't get the support and encouragement she needed to go forward in her spiritual life. "I lived in the inner city, and every Sunday I'd walk to another church to check it out. I kept looking and seeking to know more about God," she said, "but I couldn't find what I needed."

Jackie needed a relationship with God, but she also needed to experience love, security, and affirmation in her personal life. "My family broke up when I was seven," she related. "I did not even see my father as I was growing up, and I missed that." Jackie's grief over losing the relationship with her father intensified in her teen years as she experienced even more hurts in her life. There was a catch in her throat, and her voice grew soft, as she talked about those years. "When I look back on my teen years I remember more pain and heartache than I can sometimes bear to think about," she recalled. "I was the victim of a lot of abuse. Emotional, physical, and sexual." She felt betrayed by people she had trusted to love and care for her. "Through this time of trauma, I knew there was a God, and I believed that he cared for me," she said. "I just couldn't make sense of what was happening in my life."

After she was married, Jackie decided to go for counseling to help sort out her feelings. "My life was filled with so much fear," she confessed. "I struggled with panic attacks and sleepless nights as I relived in my mind the hurtful things that had happened to me." Counseling was helpful, but it didn't provide the spiritual answers she needed. "I knew I should be going to church," she remarked, "but my anxiety and panic attacks kept me away." At that point in her life her father died, and in desperation she cried out to God from the steps of her front porch.

The answer to her cry came a couple of days later when her neighbor Connie stopped by for a visit. The two young women talked about life and death, about families, and about Jackie's expected child. Then Connie told Jackie about a Bible study she was attending. If Jackie was interested, they could go together. "I was very interested," Jackie said. "I had prayed that God would help me find him in a deeper way, and I believed this was an answer to my prayer."

That fall Jackie went to Coffee Break with Connie. Each week the women put their little ones in car seats and drove several miles to the church. "Connie and I got to be good friends that year," Jackie remembered. "Right from the start we decided to have an open and honest friendship. I'm a black woman with a French heritage. Connie is white and her roots are Dutch. But we became dear friends—sisters in the Lord." God's answer to Jackie's cry came, in part, as Connie lived out her faith in love. Their friendship continued even after Connie and her husband moved out of state, for relationships in the Lord cross color lines, state lines, and time lines. In Christ we are one.

In her Coffee Break small group, Jackie experienced the oneness in Christ she had been seeking. "Ever since accepting Christ as a young person I had wanted to grow spiritually," she said. "Coffee Break gave me that opportunity, and I thought it was wonderful." Meeting weekly with a group of women was the right setting to nurture Jackie's faith. At Coffee Break she was encouraged to look at her life in the light of God's Word, and as she searched the Scriptures she found hope and comfort. Although she still struggled with her fears and panic attacks, she now had spiritual resources to give her strength and a group of women who prayed for her. "The Coffee Break women were jewels," she recalled gratefully. "They helped me move through a lot of junk that was still left in my life. I saw Christ in them, and I wanted that for myself." In time Jackie and her family began attending church on Sundays. "It wasn't always easy," she recalled, "but I kept coming. The church loved and accepted me—a broken black lady. I loved and accepted them as well. My church family and I were equally blessed." God's grace flowed from one to the other and back again. Jackie's prayers were being answered.

When God's children call to God for help, he hears and answers their cry, often far more abundantly than they expected. Jackie cried out for "someone or something" that would reveal God's presence in her life. In answer to that call, God provided a Christian friend who listened and loved. God led her to a small group of women who prayed and provided. She found a church home where she was enfolded and taught the truth of God's Word. But most importantly, God answered her cry by providing his presence. God's Word brought understanding, and with that understanding came comfort and peace. "I sometimes have my bad days," Jackie said. "But I know what to do when I feel afraid. I just go back to Jesus and ask him to wrap his arms around me. I call out God's promises and claim God's peace." Today she says, "I'm right where I always wanted to be—nestled in God's arms, and giving him praise."

Prayer

Lord, listen to your children praying. Hear our cries for help. And Lord, use me to be an answer to someone's cry. Give me a heart that loves, ears that listen, hands that help. May someone see you through me today so that your name is exalted. Amen.

God's Perfect Plan

*This is what the L*ORD *says: "When seventy years are completed for Babylon, I will come to you and fulfill my gracious promise to bring you back to this place. For I know the plans I have for you," declares the L*ORD*, "plans to prosper you and not to harm you, plans to give you hope and a future. Then you will call upon me and come and pray to me, and I will listen to you. You will seek me and find me when you seek me with all your heart. I will be found by you," declares the L*ORD*, "and will bring you back from captivity."*

—Jeremiah 29:10-14

The phone rang while Diane was giving a late-afternoon piano lesson. The social worker on the line asked if Diane could come and pick up a little girl whose mother was admitting herself into an alcohol treatment program. The mother needed someone to watch her two-year-old, and she had given the worker Diane's name and number. Puzzled, Diane searched her memory, but she didn't know this mother and child. Besides, she was pretty busy at the moment. Her initial reaction was to say, "Sorry, I can't do this," but Diane loved little children. Two-year-olds in particular had a special place in her heart, for she had been teaching the twos in Story Hour for some time now. She had a two-year-old of her own, and she kept thinking how desperate a mother would need to be to hand her toddler over to a stranger. Somehow the Holy Spirit moved Diane to say, "Yes. I'll come and get her." And God's plan for little Gina's life began to unfold.

Gina's first visit lasted only three days, but it was long enough for Diane's whole family to fall in love with her. When Gina's mother walked away from treatment, she called to ask for her daughter to be returned. Reluctantly Diane obeyed that request. In caring for Gina, Diane had noticed signs of neglect and abuse, and she knew she needed to stay in touch with this family. She offered to care for Gina one day a week. "Would Tuesday be a good day?" she asked. That was the day she taught the two-year-olds in her church's Story Hour program, and Diane knew it would be a wonderful place to teach Gina about Jesus in a way perfectly suited for her age.

If you are a Story Hour teacher, or if you've ever taught very young children in another setting, you know how rewarding it can be to spend time each week with preschoolers. But you also know how much work is involved. Little Lambs and Story Hour teachers make lesson plans, prepare stories, organize crafts, arrange activities, and plan to arrive early on Story Hour mornings. Diane fine-tuned her routine with her four children, getting the older ones off to school, keeping her two-year-old content, and staying on schedule so that she could pick up Gina on Tuesday mornings.

One Tuesday Diane's youngest was ill, and finding child care for him took more time than she had figured. She would have called Gina's mom to cancel, but Gina's family had no phone. Rushing against the clock, she drove onto the freeway and discovered a massive traffic jam. "Now I'll really be late," she thought. In frustration she put her head on the steering wheel and cried out, "God, what kind of plan is this? Does any of this make sense? I can't figure it out." To pass the time as she waited for traffic to clear, Diane turned on the radio. The words of a gospel song seemed to be a direct answer to her cry to God:

We have this moment to hold in our hands
and to touch as it slips through our fingers like sand;
yesterday's gone and tomorrow may never come,
but we have this moment today.

—"We Have This Moment Today." Words by Gloria Gaither, © 1975 Gaither Music Company ASCAP. All rights reserved. Used by permission.

It seemed like God was right there in the car, telling her to trust him. She couldn't do anything about the past, and she didn't know about the future, but God was giving her today. Another day with Gina, another day with the two-year-olds in Story Hour, another day with God. He had a plan and he was in control.

Like Diane, you probably experience frustration about things beyond your control—time crunches, traffic, sick kids, unexpected interruptions. Things may often seem to go wrong, especially on the days you are volunteering your time to serve others. If you're a Story Hour leader, you may wonder why the children who need Story Hour the most miss so often or move away or misbehave. Diane found her answer in recognizing God's control, in accepting that God was providing the strength she needed for each day. We don't know whether we'll have our Story Hour kids back for another week. We don't know if the women will be back for the next Coffee Break lesson. But we do know that we have "this moment today."

Gina moved through the Story Hour years, spending more time with Diane and her family. When she was ready for school and could no longer attend Story Hour, Diane suggested Sundays as the day for Gina to visit, and their physical and spiritual bonds deepened. But even as the foundation was being laid for Gina's faith, her parental home was crumbling. Neglected and often left alone in her home, Gina treasured the times with her "other family." She began to ask, "Can I stay for a couple more hours?" Then, "Can I stay another day?" Conditions in her parental home deteriorated, and efforts to hold the mother and child together were fruitless. When Gina's safety was compromised and her home life no longer tolerable, Gina came to live with Diane's family in foster care.

During these years, the words from Jeremiah 29:11 often came to Diane's mind. A favorite verse for many years, the truth of these words now had a greater impact: "For I know the plans I have for you . . . plans to give you hope and a future." Over the years, hope for Gina had often dimmed, and the future seemed uncertain. Diane needed to do what we all need to do—trust the Master Planner. Nine years after Diane received the phone call asking her to come and pick up a little girl, Diane and her husband legally adopted Gina. One of the factors that helped the judge approve the adoption decision was the album of photos Diane had taken of Gina with Diane's family, the earliest pictures taken in Story Hour when Gina was a toddler. A few months later Gina was baptized and made profession of faith in the sanctuary above the room where she had discovered Jesus' love in Story Hour. The Scripture read that day was Jeremiah 29:11.

Story Hour is part of God's plan for thousands of preschoolers today. If you are a teacher of little ones, treasure the moments that God gives you as you lay a foundation of faith in their lives. Can a child seek and find the Lord in Story Hour? Yes she can!

Prayer

Lord, I am so grateful that you have a plan for my life, and for the precious children in Little Lambs and Story Hour. Help me to trust you for each moment of each day. Amen.

Open Our Eyes, Lord

As they talked and discussed these things with each other, Jesus himself came up and walked along with them; but they were kept from recognizing him. . . . Beginning with Moses and all the Prophets, he explained to them what was said in all the Scriptures concerning himself. . . .

Then their eyes were opened and they recognized him. . . . They asked each other, "Were not our hearts burning within us while he talked with us on the road and opened the Scriptures to us?"

—Luke 24:15-16, 27, 31-32

The shy thirteen-year-old slowly walked to the front of the Jewish synagogue and climbed the steps to the podium. Today was her *bat mitzvah*, her special confirmation ceremony. She had prepared for this day since she was five years old by attending Hebrew school twice a week. Now she was ready to lead the congregation and invited guests through the service in Hebrew. She found the appointed place in the Hebrew text and began to read: *"Shema yisraēl adonai elohēnu adonai echad."* "Hear, O Israel: The LORD our God, the LORD is one." As Marla read the words her audience nodded their heads in approval. Today's ceremony meant that Marla was now a member of the adult Jewish community, and her family was very proud.

"I come from a very close-knit, conservative Jewish family," Marla told me. "We kept the Sabbath, attended synagogue, and observed Jewish holidays and festivals." The small Midwestern town where Marla was raised provided a comfortable setting for her childhood and youth. "My sisters and I had a very secure home life," she said. "I remember lots of happiness." But when Marla was nineteen, her father died. His death changed the family structure and brought stress into the family's life. "The year after he died we followed very strict religious traditions in connection with mourning," she recalled. "We grieved our loss deeply." By this time Marla had entered college, and, while still embracing Judaism, she discovered new dimensions in her life. She fell in love with a young man who was not Jewish and they decided to marry.

"Richard was raised as a Catholic," she said. "We chose a simple, nonreligious wedding ceremony, and we decided to each keep our own faith." However, as time went on, religion became less of a priority in their lives. "Basically we just celebrated the holidays with our respective families," she noted. "For the most part, we didn't see a need for anything spiritual." But when their second daughter, Jaclyn, was born with a serious heart defect, the young couple recognized that their lives had a spiritual vacuum. Marla's voice grew softer as she remembered that difficult time.

"Jaclyn needed surgery when she was one month old," she continued. "We realized the seriousness of her condition, but we were uncertain where to turn for spiritual help." When baby Jaclyn did not survive the surgery, Richard and Marla were faced with a dilemma. "Where do you go for comfort at a time like this?" Marla asked. "Who should we ask to help us bring closure to such a difficult loss?" They held a funeral service, but Marla remembers, "Something was missing. We comforted each other, but I didn't know how to reach out to God."

About a year later a job transfer took them to a new city. Marla remembers this as a difficult move. "We had no relatives, no friends, no church or synagogue. The first year was very lonely." Then a new family moved into the neighborhood, and Marla met Janet. "I am basically quiet and a little shy," Marla said. "Janet is bubbly and very outgoing. I liked her right away, and we became instant friends." The weeks turned to months and the two women developed their friendship at the kitchen table, sharing coffee and conversation. One day Janet mentioned her belief in Jesus, and Marla replied, "I'm Jewish." That was fine with Janet, but it didn't stop her from talking about her friend Jesus, who, as Janet put it, "was Jewish too."

Marla and Janet continued their kitchen table conversations. "We often ended up discussing religion," Marla recalled. "I realized that Janet knew more about the Jews in the Bible than I did. I had learned to read Hebrew, and I could recite an entire Hebrew service from memory, but I didn't have a clue what this meant for my everyday life." Then one day Janet invited Marla to a Bible study. She emphasized the opportunity for friendship and the Story Hour for Marla's little girl, Julia, but Marla resisted. "I was Jewish, and I was content to keep it that way," she said. However, Janet kept up the invitations to Coffee Break. Finally Marla agreed. "I decided the only resolution to Janet's persistent invitations was to give the group a try."

Marla attended Coffee Break reluctantly at first. "It took awhile for the comfort level to build," she remembered. But gradually she made friends, and slowly spiritual truths made their way to her heart. "I asked lots of questions," she said. "I kept asking 'Why?' and 'Where is that?' It was important to me to know where the answers were coming from." God provided for Marla's spiritual quest in unique ways at that time. Marla's husband worked nights, and she had her evenings available to study the Bible. One of the Coffee Break leaders bought her a Bible with footnotes, and Marla searched the Old Testament as she studied the New. One day Janet asked her, "What are you looking for in a Messiah?" Marla replied, "One who would redeem Israel. A king who would save his people." Janet responded, "Doesn't that sound like Jesus?" Then she added, "Don't take my word for it. Ask God to give you the truth."

Marla considered the realization that Jesus could be the Messiah. But she worried that if she accepted Jesus as God she would be guilty of blasphemy. "It was a hard barrier for me to cross," she remembered. During this time of spiritual struggle Marla discovered that she was pregnant. With the pregnancy came fear and pain as memories of Jaclyn's birth and death returned to her heart and mind. But God had put Marla in a good place for these nine months—she was part of a Coffee Break group, and the love and prayers of the group supported her. Marla prayed too. Not just for the health of her unborn baby, but for truth to be revealed. "If Jesus was really Lord, a miracle of faith had to be born in my heart," she said. "I prayed that my eyes would be open to the truth."

Marla, her husband, Richard, and their daughter Julia welcomed a healthy baby girl into their family circle. Coffee Break members, church friends, and the pastor responded with meals, visits, and an outpouring of love. This physical birth was followed a few days later by spiritual birth as Marla accepted Jesus as her Lord and Savior and was born again. Richard and Marla stood side by side to profess their faith in Jesus Christ, and Marla and her infant daughter, Amanda, were baptized together.

As Marla looks back over her life, she recognizes that Jesus was there all the time. "It took a while for my eyes to be opened," she said. "But now I can see that the Lord was walking with me long before I recognized him." Marla's advice to all who will listen is this: "Don't be afraid to tell others about your faith in Jesus. And if they resist, be willing to pray and persist. I'm glad Janet did that for me."

Prayer

Dear Jesus, how I love you. Thank you for revealing yourself through your Word and your Spirit. Open my eyes to see you and give me courage and conviction to share my faith in you. Amen.

Sharing the Riches of Christ

Although I am less than the least of all God's people, this grace was given me: to preach to the Gentiles the unsearchable riches of Christ, and to make plain to everyone the administration of this mystery, which for ages past was kept hidden in God, who created all things.

—*Ephesians 3:8-9*

One by one the women entered the church fellowship room, found seats around the table, and opened their Bibles to the gospel of John. Sooja also found her place and quietly waited to see if her questions about faith would be answered. She was new to the Korean small group Bible study, but she wasn't new to the Bible. "I was born and raised in a Christian family in Korea," she said. "But even though I went to church all my life, I never had assurance of my salvation. Faith was never talked about; it was just assumed." The failure to find assurance left Sooja with the feeling that something was missing. "By the time I reached age forty and was living in the United States, I knew something was wrong with the spiritual side of my life. I knew God as creator," she said, "but where did Jesus fit in?"

In her desire to find the truth, Sooja went through a period of soul-searching, asking all her friends, "How can I know if I have faith?" Her friends gave her lots of answers, but no one pointed her to the gospel. One day a friend invited her to a small group Bible study, and Sooja told herself, "Now I'll get to find out who Jesus really is."

Sooja asked lots and lots of questions as the group discussed the gospel of John. Myung, the small group leader, and other class members were always ready to help Sooja in her quest for spiritual knowledge. The questions kept coming as Sooja sought to fill her hunger for God. Then one day Myung asked if she and the coleader could visit Sooja at her home, and a date was set. Sooja recalled that day. "When Myung rang the bell I answered it, eager to be a good hostess. But Myung asked me, 'Where will *you* be most comfortable?' I smile to remember it, because she was thinking of my comfort." The three women chose to sit around the coffee table in the family room.

"We sat the Oriental way—on the floor," Sooja remembered. "We were sitting very close together, and I could tell Myung was serious." In preparation for the visit, Myung had tucked a little booklet called *The Four Spiritual*

Laws into her purse. Now she took it out and began to share with Sooja the concepts of God's love, humanity's sin, and God's provision in Jesus Christ. When they got to the part about receiving Christ, Myung asked, "Do you want to pray and accept Jesus as Lord of your life?" "Oh, yes," Sooja replied. "That's what I've been looking for." The women prayed together, seated on the floor around the coffee table. As they were praying, tears began to drip onto the table. "Where are those tears coming from?" Sooja wondered. And then she realized, "They are my tears."

Sooja shed those tears of joy as the Holy Spirit "made plain the mystery" of new life in Christ. "At last," she thought, "I *know* who Jesus is. He's my Savior and Lord." With that assurance came a hunger to know more about God. When the other women left, Sooja sat down on the couch and began to read the Bible, beginning with Genesis. By the time her children arrived home from school that day, she had read straight through to Deuteronomy. This was the beginning of a disciplined search for "the unsearchable riches of Christ," for she wanted to know God's will and be open to whatever God had planned for her life. And God did have wonderful things planned for Sooja, as he does for all his children. Doors of leadership opened one after the other, generally with small groups of Korean women who came and asked Sooja to be their Bible leader. God was preparing Sooja "to make plain to everyone the . . . mystery, which for ages past was kept hidden in God."

A unique opportunity to "share the riches in Christ" came when Sooja started a Bible study with a group of Korean women temporarily living in the States while their husbands completed work assignments for Korean-based companies. These young wives were looking for something to occupy their time, and they welcomed the invitation to Coffee Break. Most of the women were from Buddhist or atheist backgrounds. They had never studied the Bible before, and they knew little or nothing about God or Jesus. But they were eager to learn. After a couple of months of studying together, one of the women asked if Sooja would come to her home. When Sooja rang the bell, two young women were eagerly awaiting her visit. Like her mentor, Myung, Sooja had tucked a copy of *The Four Spiritual Laws* into her purse, and she was ready to present the challenge to accept Christ as Savior and Lord. "The women were ready also—ready to receive Christ," she said. "The Bible study had prepared their hearts, and they opened the door not just to me but to Jesus."

That visit took place several years ago. Sooja continues to offer Coffee Break Bible study to the Korean women in her community, and she is enthusiastic about the dynamics of small groups. "The women ask questions and share freely. I watch the expressions on their faces. That tells me when they are ready to accept Christ." Sooja is always prepared to share the gospel one on one, and she carries her copy of *The Four Spiritual Laws* with her. "Almost every time we study a Coffee Break book, one or two of the women accept Christ," she said. "When we studied *Discover Genesis*, I thought it would not be evangelistic, but three women received Jesus as Savior because of the study." Often those who have become Christians are transferred with their husbands to countries all around the world. They leave the small group, taking Christ with them to every corner of the globe. Many are determined to start their own small group Bible study in their new community, and they stay in touch with Sooja. And so God's plan to make plain the riches of Christ is carried out as one woman shares with another, and then another, and another.

Each one of us can be part of God's evangelism plan by sharing Christ with others. If that seems like an overwhelming task, remember that God has promised to provide whatever you need, including the words to say as you tell others of his love (Matt. 7:7). The first step is to make certain that you personally know God's love, and that you have received him as your Lord and Savior. The prayer that follows is one you can use to invite Christ to come into your life; it is also a prayer that you can share.

Prayer

Dear Jesus, I need you in my life. I confess my sins and ask for forgiveness. Thank you for your promise to be my Savior and Lord. I open my heart to you. Come in and make me the person you want me to be. Amen.

Seek and You Will Find

"Ask and it will be given to you; seek and you will find; knock and the door will be opened to you. For everyone who asks receives; he who seeks finds; and to him who knocks, the door will be opened."

—Matthew 7:7-8

Mary pulled the weekly newspaper out of the mailbox and slowly walked back into the house. She sat down and turned to the section titled "Things to Do and Places to Go." Ever since moving to this suburban neighborhood Mary had been searching for something. The job transfer that her husband, Chris, had accepted meant a lot of changes for their little family. Most of these changes were good. Chris liked his new job, they had a lovely home, the baby had settled into a reasonable routine, and life in the suburbs was comfortable. But Mary felt that something was missing. She just couldn't pinpoint it. "I knew very few of my neighbors," she said. "I tried attending a local church, but I never connected. In my heart I knew there had to be more, but I didn't know how to find it. So I kept looking."

Mary and Chris are like thousands of families in communities scattered across the United States and Canada. Job transfers often provide people with better houses and more comfortable lifestyles, but the moves disconnect families and friends and leave people looking for meaning in life. The search for "something more" kept Mary checking the local paper. One day she noticed a small ad for a Bible study that held promise. It had been placed by the Coffee Break Bible study of a local church, and it ran weekly. Mary was especially drawn by the wording: "Open to all women. No previous knowledge needed. Free nursery."

"This sounded great," Mary said. "I really wanted to go, but taking the first step wasn't easy. I kept putting if off, but each week I looked to see if the invitation was still in the paper."

Then one week the ad changed. It was the Lenten season, and the Coffee Break program planned a special event called "Bloom Where You Are Planted." This captured Mary's attention, and she called to register Adam for the nursery and herself for the coffee hour. When the appointed date arrived, Mary started questioning the wisdom of going someplace where she didn't know a soul. "What if no one is friendly?" she asked herself. "What if Adam doesn't like the nursery?" As she was hesitating the phone rang. The call was from a friend in another city—a friend who had given Adam a Bible when he was christened. Inscribed on the front cover of that Bible was the phrase "Bloom where you are planted." That phone call from her friend was the nudge Mary needed. She had a sense of peace, and she knew she would go.

Mary's apprehensions dissolved completely as she entered the church and discovered a warm and friendly group of women. When one of the greeters read Mary's name tag, she recalled her phone registration and inquired about Adam. "That won my heart," Mary remembered. "I was so impressed that someone cared enough to remember my child's name. I knew that coming was the right decision, and I decided to return for the group study the next week."

Special events can often be the entrance to Bible studies or to church attendance. A nonthreatening topic with broad appeal provides an opportunity for a seeker to "check out" a group without making a long-term commitment. The fact that Mary felt comfortable at the event was no accident. Coffee Break leaders had prayed, planned, and prepared for this day. God was at work in Mary's heart, but the leaders needed to work too, as they obeyed Jesus' command to "Ask . . . seek . . . and knock." Laying a foundation of prayer was as critical as choosing a speaker or preparing the refreshments and decorations.

The very next week Mary joined the Coffee Break Bible study group. "I liked it from the start," she recalled. "There was a mixture of women from a variety of backgrounds and ages, and it didn't matter that I had never studied the Bible before. I learned so much from the other women that I was eager to continue."

The good experience at Coffee Break prompted Mary and her husband, Chris, to visit the church on Sunday. "There was a nursery for Adam, a small group Bible class, and lots of friendly people," Mary recalled. She and Chris decided to keep coming. "We both attended church as children, but we came from different religious traditions, and this was a new experience for us." The Sunday school class they attended used the same Discover Your Bible study materials as Coffee Break used. "It was the perfect place to discover the truths of God's Word," Chris remembered. "We had so much to learn, and we could learn it together as a couple." Soon Chris also began attending Men's Life, a Bible study for men, where he was able to apply what he was learning to his personal life.

Week after week Chris and Mary studied and discussed the Bible, and week after week their spiritual understanding deepened. "Both of us had heard the gospel read in church," Mary said, "but the connection to personal salvation was never made. We knew God was important, but God was up there, and we were down here." Gradually, as they learned more through their participation in Coffee Break, Men's Life, and Sunday church services, Chris and Mary realized that Christ's gift of salvation was for them. They accepted Jesus as their Savior, professed their faith in him, and became active members of their church. They were eager to find ways to serve God and share their faith.

Coffee Break often becomes the bridge to church membership, and many pastors are grateful for the role of evangelism in Coffee Break Bible studies. But it takes a church to effectively enfold a family into fellowship. The small group that Chris and Mary attended each Sunday became the place where they were assimilated, discipled, and connected to the church. That first Lenten coffee was the entrance, Coffee Break the bridge, the small group the discipler, and the church a place to serve and grow.

New Christians have a wonderful enthusiasm for sharing Christ. Mary invited neighbors to Coffee Break, Chris became part of the evangelism team, and both looked for ways to use their newly discovered spiritual gifts. Then Chris broke the news that he was being transferred to another job—out of state and far from Coffee Break, Men's Life, the small group, and their church. It had been only two years since Mary and Adam had first come to Coffee Break, and the leaders and members were not ready to release them. But God's hand was on their lives, and the two years had been the foundation they needed. "We came to you as seekers," Mary told the Coffee Break staff. "We are leaving having found a Savior."

Today Chris, Mary, and their family are serving the Lord in a new community and are growing in their faith. They remember the two years in their former church with fondness. "We will never forget you," Mary wrote to her Coffee Break group after she moved. "You opened our eyes to the Lord."

Prayer

Father God, I thank you for the promise of "Ask, seek, knock." Today I ask that I will be a seeker of those who need to be found. Thank you for opening the door of salvation to all who knock in Jesus' name. Amen.

Living Water for a Thirsty Soul

As the rain and the snow

come down from heaven,

and do not return to it

without watering the earth

and making it bud and flourish,

so that it yields seed for the sower and bread for the eater,

so is my word that goes out from my mouth:

It will not return to me empty,

but will accomplish what I desire

and achieve the purpose for which I sent it.

—Isaiah 55:10-11

It was a sunny day in spring. Finally the winter snows were gone, the rains had halted, and the time was right to get out the stroller for a walk with the baby. Carol and her husband were new to this part of New England. They had moved here when John accepted his first job after college. Carol enjoyed being a "stay-at-home mom," and she looked forward to these outings—after all, walking was healthy, the baby enjoyed the stroll, and it was inexpensive recreation. It was fun to see the flowers in her neighbors' yards, and these walks were a good way to make new friends.

Carol met a neighbor who also pushed a stroller, and the two soon discovered the joys of walking and talking together. As Carol and Karen walked they talked about their lives, sharing dreams as well as difficulties. One day the topic of Bible study came up. Karen was attending a study group in a nearby church. Would Carol like to try it? There was a wonderful nursery for the babies, it was fun, and it was free. While Carol never thought of herself as "nonreligious," she wasn't ready to go to some "silly Bible study," so she turned down Karen's invitation. "Maybe someday," she thought, "but not today, thanks just the same." Meanwhile the talks and walks with the strollers continued. So did the invitations to try the Bible study. As Karen persisted in asking her friend to Coffee Break, Carol resisted—for a whole year. Finally Carol decided she would give it a try, but she determined that she would *not* be a pushover. She was an independent thinker. "No one is going to cram anything down my throat," she told herself.

At Coffee Break Carol asked lots of questions—difficult questions that challenged the leaders. "During the week as I worked through my lesson I would think of questions I knew the leaders couldn't answer just so I could see their response," she said. Carol's presence at Coffee Break put a new focus into the leaders' prayer times as they considered how they would handle her hard questions. Carol was accepted, listened to, and loved. The small group setting of

Coffee Break provided a safe place to express her doubts and ask questions, and Carol kept coming.

Even though Carol faithfully attended Coffee Break for over a year, she resisted putting her faith in Christ. She struggled with her doubts about a personal God, and even expressed a fascination with the Baha'i religion. Her leaders prayed consistently, took time for one-on-one conversations, presented the gospel, and waited for the Holy Spirit's timing. They were available to share the truth and to show love, and Carol's consistent questioning didn't put them off.

Although Carol didn't realize it, God was working mightily in her life. Just as the rain and snow had watered the earth, bringing the spring flowers Carol enjoyed, so too God's Word was watering her thirsty soul, preparing it for the truths that would blossom there. God promised through the prophet Isaiah that the word that goes out "will not return to me empty." God's purpose would be achieved, and as Carol's rebellious spirit softened under the gentle rain of truth, seeds began to take root and grow.

Coffee Break leaders have often marveled at the workings of the Holy Spirit as he brings people to faith. "My thoughts are not your thoughts, neither are your ways my ways," declares the Lord (Isa. 55:8). Sometimes God moves in a mysterious way to bring our thoughts in line with his. Carol experienced the mysterious and powerful working of God's way in her life about two years after beginning her Coffee Break journey when a lovely summer day turned into near tragedy. Her seventeen-month-old daughter, Lesley, was rushed to the hospital following a serious injury. Lesley came close to death, and now Carol sat alone at her little girl's bedside. Terrified by the possible loss of her daughter, Carol cried out, "God, if you are real, I want to know." At that moment, alone in the room with her injured child, Carol felt two hands on her shoulders. "There was no physical explanation for the touch," Carol recalled. "No one else was in the room. But I *knew* I was not alone." Carol had felt the presence of the Lord.

That moment marked a turning point in Carol's life. Her questions and doubts melted away like snow in the spring sunshine. The weeks and months of Coffee Break lessons had prepared her heart for faith, and she accepted Jesus as Lord and Savior. Lesley recovered from her injuries, and Carol returned to Coffee Break in the fall with a story to tell. As Carol's husband, John, observed her response to God's presence in her life, he also surrendered his life to Christ. They professed their faith in Jesus, and their two daughters were baptized in the church where Carol attended Coffee Break.

Carol continued to ask questions in Coffee Break, but she no longer played "stump the leader." Now her questions were tools for transforming her life. Carol grew in her faith. In time she was asked to be an assistant leader of a group, then a leader, and eventually she directed her church's Coffee Break program. When New England was chosen as the site of the 1998 Coffee Break convention, Carol was chosen as the chairperson. She had come a long way on her faith journey, from resistance to acceptance to fruitfulness. Carol's thirst for truth had led her to the living water, and the result is a life that has bloomed for God's glory.

Carol's story is an encouragement to every woman whose friend continues to turn down invitations to Coffee Break. It is an encouragement to every leader who has a "difficult questioner" in her small group. It is an encouragement to every church that has hosted a Coffee Break ministry and wondered about "the results." God works in his own time and in his own way, but God does work. While we can see the results of the rain that waters the earth, we do not always see the harvest that God's Word produces. But the written Word applied to people's hearts by the power of the Holy Spirit provides the thirst-quenching water of which Jesus spoke—the water that wells up to eternal life.

Prayer

Lord, you have shown your faithfulness in the rain and the snow that bring the fruit and the flower. Give me the faith to persevere in ministry even when I do not see the results, knowing that you have promised that your Word will not return empty. Amen.

A New Song

I waited patiently for the LORD;

he turned to me and heard my cry.

He put a new song in my mouth,

a hymn of praise to our God.

Many will see and fear

and put their trust in the LORD.

—Psalm 40:1, 3

Laurie lay on the couch in the darkened living room with the blinds closed and the door locked. Her two young children played amidst the clutter in the room, but Laurie was too depressed to pay much attention to them or to the clutter. A black cloud hung over her, and in her heart she did not want to go on living. As Laurie recalled this period of her life, she told me, "I felt like I wasn't a good wife, I wasn't a good mother. I was worthless." Married very young, Laurie was overwhelmed by her circumstances. She had a hard time coping with life. With no spiritual resources to draw on, Laurie felt her hopeless situation must be her destiny. "I knew there was a God," she said, "but I was certain he had forgotten about me. Even though I had heard of Jesus, I didn't think he would personally touch my life. I was a very depressed young woman and didn't see a way out."

Laurie's depression had pushed her to the point of wanting to give up. It was difficult for her to care for her children and to relate to her husband. "My husband and I always shared a love of music," she stated. "In my depression, I tried to push everything away—including music and my marriage. There was no song in my heart, only darkness." As she lay on the couch she told herself, "There must be something better than this, but what is it?"

Laurie had kept her depression hidden for long time, but there was one person with whom she was honest. That person was her friend Gail. The two women had been introduced by Laurie's husband, Dave. Dave and Gail's husband, Dusty, were cab drivers and worked for the same company in their midwestern Canadian community. Laurie and Gail had children the same age, and the women soon became good friends. Gail had been attending a Coffee Break Bible study for several years, and it had changed her life. "In Coffee Break I came to know the Lord," Gail told Laurie. "I always thought I wasn't good enough to be a Christian, but through Coffee Break I discovered that Jesus accepts you right where you are." Gail knew that Coffee Break was just the right place for Laurie too.

Gail often talked to Laurie about Coffee Break. She told her that the women she met there had the same problems and struggles the two of them experienced. But the Coffee Break women had something else besides—they had peace. At first Laurie resisted Gail's invitations to attend the Bible study. "Christians are plastic people," she told Gail. "They may be friendly on the outside, but underneath the smiles there'll be the same rejection I've always experienced." Gail was patiently persistent. "It's working for me," she told Laurie. "Won't you at least give it a try?"

Eventually Laurie did decide to go to Coffee Break, but she also decided not to make any changes in how she looked or acted. "I'm not going to get dressed up. I won't even wash my hair. These women are going to have to take me just as I am." So Laurie dressed down. She smoked on the steps of the church just to see how the other women would react. She pulled out all the defense mechanisms that had worked in the past. "I did everything I could to offend them," she remembered, "but the group still accepted me and loved me." Gradually her resistance broke down, and she began to see the love of Jesus in the outstretched hands of the Coffee Break women. "If the women who represented Jesus accepted me, then Jesus also accepted me," she confessed. "Little by little Jesus drew me to himself, and I put my trust in him."

Like Gail, Laurie experienced the love of God as she studied the Bible and met with her small group. The more she trusted Jesus, the easier it was to trust other people. The acceptance she received at Coffee Break gave her courage to attend church, where she continued to grow. Laurie's problems did not go away. But she was able to face the challenges and responsibilities in her life with new strength and courage.

Laurie continued to attend Coffee Break, and her husband joined her in attending church services. Hungry for the things of God, Laurie had found a place to be fed and filled, and her depression lifted. Her love for music found new expression when she was asked to be the music leader for Coffee Break. Then Dave was invited to sing for a worship service at church, and soon they were part of the church's praise team. "After we committed our lives to Christ," Laurie said, "I felt like we had been set on fire from within. We were both very eager to know more of God and happy to be involved in the activity of the church." A new song was emerging in their hearts and lives, and they felt the Lord was leading them into a music ministry.

One day Laurie and Dave called Gail and Dusty to ask if they would listen to a song they were preparing to perform. Although Dusty attended church on occasion, he had never made a personal commitment to Christ. But that day Dave and Laurie played a song that touched Dusty's heart, and he knew he wanted the same faith that his wife and friends shared. "It had been fourteen years since I had found the Lord through Coffee Break," Gail said. Now the circle was complete.

Today both couples are active in church and ministry. Gail and Dusty participate in the church where Gail attends Coffee Break. Laurie and Dave have their own music ministry, writing and recording praise and worship songs. "Our music ministry is aimed at people who are outside the walls of the church," Laurie said. "We are taking the message of God's grace to a lost world, bringing light to those in darkness." Laurie and Dave and Gail and Dusty have found a new song to sing—the song of the redeemed. Their stories celebrate the wonderful ways God works through our friendships, our families, our circumstances. They remind us to be persistent in asking a friend to Coffee Break. They remind us to pray faithfully for the salvation of our family and friends. And they remind us that God will work in our lives in his own time.

If there is no song in your heart today, ask the Lord to give you "a new song." He is able to do far more than we ask or think. Then pray about an opportunity to share your song with someone who needs to hear about God's love.

Prayer

Father, let there be a song in my heart today. Give me grace to share that song with those I meet in the name of Jesus. Amen.

Trust in the Lord

Trust in the LORD *with all your heart*

and lean not on your own understanding;

in all your ways acknowledge him,

and he will make your paths straight.

—*Proverbs 3:5-6*

The tea kettle in the church kitchen whistled cheerfully as Ellen finished setting out the scones and jam for the Christmas coffee. As she looked around the room she mentally checked off the items that had been prepared for the guests. Cups and saucers, napkins, scones, and Scottish shortbread—all were in place right next to the new Coffee Break brochures. This morning the women of Cumbernauld, Scotland, would receive an invitation to Coffee Break Bible study, along with their coffee or tea. Ellen smiled as she thought of the stack of name tags she'd purposely left at home. "Forget the name tags," the church ladies had told her. "No one will wear them." "Then how will we get acquainted?" Ellen had asked. "We'll have a 'wee blether' and everything will be fine," the women replied. A "wee blether," Ellen discovered, was a little chat. It went along with the scones and the tea. Ellen breathed a silent prayer, "Lord, I'm trusting you today to provide a 'wee blether' and perhaps a bit more." It seemed to Ellen that since moving to Scotland she had learned to trust the Lord for just about everything.

The previous year Ellen and her family had been transplanted from sunny Southern California to Cumbernauld, Scotland, a town a few miles outside of Glasgow. "When my husband told me he felt called to return to his native Scotland as a missionary pastor, I had some apprehensive moments," Ellen related. "But God softened my heart and gave me the peace I needed to make this major move." Some of that peace was provided by the support of Ellen's Coffee Break group in California. "They encouraged me, prayed for me, and shared my excitement," she recalled. "They definitely were a part of God's plan for my life as I prepared my family for our move."

"I had been attending Coffee Break for about three years, and I loved it," Ellen said. "I was invited during a time of spiritual struggle in my life, and the small group was the perfect place for the healing and comfort I needed." Coffee Break provided a loving atmosphere and warm fellowship, and it allowed Ellen to be nurtured by a study of God's Word. "I grew spiritually as I searched the truth in Scripture and shared my discoveries with the group," she reflected. "As I look back on those years of Coffee Break, I realize now that God used that time to prepare me for leadership overseas." While Ellen was in Coffee Break, her preschool children attended Story Hour and Little Lambs, where they too were encouraged in faith and with prayer. "This program ministered to our entire family," she said. "I felt that God would use it in Scotland in some way."

The opportunity to start a Coffee Break ministry didn't come right away. Life in Cumbernauld was quite different from life in California. "We had a lot of adjustments to make the first year," Ellen recalled. "We needed to adapt our American ways to the Scottish style. The Scots are much more reserved than Southern Californians, and while we all speak English, our family was the one with the accent." Ellen began to build relationships with the women in her church and community.

She volunteered in an after-school ministry for community kids and watched for opportunities to connect with the parents. As she observed the families and their needs, Ellen knew the time was right to reach these moms through Coffee Break and Story Hour. "I had lots of questions," Ellen said, "the biggest one being, Can I do this?" Ellen knew that *she* couldn't, but *God* could. "It was really a matter of trust," she said. Prayer had been part of Ellen's planning even before she made her missionary move. She enlisted the prayers of her former Coffee Break group and a few women in her new community. Then it was time to approach the church board. They readily gave their approval and offered prayer support, but the rest was up to Ellen. "That's when I realized I really needed help," she said with a smile. When she sent an SOS call to her Coffee Break friends in the States they responded with a care package filled with study guides and other materials for getting a group started. "I was overwhelmed and affirmed at the same time," Ellen remembered.

The Christmas coffee was the kick-off event. "We started by inviting the moms who sent their kids to the after-school group, and we put up notices in the small shops in the town center. Most of all, we prayed." Whether you're starting a Coffee Break in Scotland, Sarnia, or Sioux City, prayer is the key. Ellen knew that God had a plan. She needed to be willing to work and to wait.

"That first season our group was small and very, very quiet," Ellen reflected. "None of the women, including the helpers, had ever been in a Bible study like this. It took a long time for them to open up." But Ellen was patient. She continued to ask the right questions, she smiled, and she prayed. "I was convinced that there was a need for Bible discovery and for personal sharing around God's Word," she stated. Ellen's confidence in God's direction kept her moving forward during the first few quiet months. Then she began to notice little changes. The women were more relaxed, they were willing to share their thoughts, and they were starting to smile more. Ellen rejoiced when a few new faces turned up in response to the notice in the town center. And then there was Rosemary.

Rosemary came to class during the first Coffee Break session and listened attentively as the group discussed Scriptures relating faith and life. God's Word is a powerful teacher, and Rosemary discovered truths that surprised her. "She began asking questions," Ellen said. "And then she acknowledged that she was not living a Christian life." However, Rosemary continued to attend the Bible study and, little by little, Ellen noticed a change in her. "I knew God was working in her heart, and one day I sensed a softness and openness that hadn't been there before." When Ellen asked her about it, tears welled up in Rosemary's eyes as she shared that she had made a commitment to surrender her life fully to Jesus Christ. Rosemary was baptized, and the week before Ellen left on furlough, Rosemary gave her testimony to the church. "Coffee Break was the turning point in my life," Rosemary said as she thanked Ellen for bringing Coffee Break to Scotland.

Ellen knew that Coffee Break in Cumbernauld was effectively bringing people into a personal, vital, and growing relationship with Jesus Christ. While home on furlough, Ellen kept in contact with her Scottish friends. "Who is leading the lessons?" she once asked. The answer—"It will be Rosemary's turn next"—warmed her heart.

Is God calling you to begin a Coffee Break ministry in your new community? Claim Ellen's favorite verse—Proverbs 3:5-6—and wait for wonderful results.

Prayer

Lord, sometimes it is so hard for me to trust the unknown. Forgive me for substituting my understanding for your guidance. I await your leading. Amen.

Fear Not, You Are Mine

"Fear not, for I have redeemed you;

I have summoned you by name; you are mine.

When you pass through the waters,

I will be with you;

and when you pass through the rivers,

they will not sweep over you.

For I am the LORD, your God,

the Holy one of Israel, your Savior."

—Isaiah 43:1-3

The year was 1975. The city of Saigon, South Vietnam, was about to fall to the Communists. The American troops had been evacuated, and Loan and her husband knew they needed to escape or they would become prisoners of war. "We heard from my husband's sister that helicopters were rescuing people from the roof of the U.S. Embassy," Loan said. "We hurried to be among those who were being airlifted to safety, but we were too late. When we got to the embassy the doors were shut." Desperate to flee, Loan and her husband took the advice of an embassy employee who told them, "Go, just go. Get to the harbor and climb on a boat, any boat. But hurry."

Loan and her husband ran to the harbor and jumped into a boat. "I could hear the shooting behind me," she recalled. "When I looked back I could see fire in the city. I was feeling sad and afraid at the same time." Tears filled her eyes as she recalled the flight from her homeland. "We left everything behind," she said softly, "and there was no time to say goodbye." Loan spent the next three days and nights in the small boat without food and water before being rescued by an American ship. The young couple eventually landed in a refugee camp in California, where they waited for a sponsor. "I was twenty-one years old," Loan said. "I had my husband, but I had nothing else. I left my father, mother, brother, sister, and my country." Loan knew she had to look forward; there was no going back now.

After spending several months in the refugee camp, Loan and her husband were sponsored by a church in western Michigan and given an opportunity to start life over in a new country. They settled down to find work and start a family. "I was raised as a Buddhist, but in America I didn't practice my religion," Loan related. "When life was good to me, I confess I didn't think I needed any religion." Loan attended beauty school and began work as a beautician. Her career and her family filled her life, and she saw no reason to make any changes. Then one day Loan had a new client, and slowly her perspective began to change.

Janet, a Coffee Break director, discovered Loan's shop through a friend's recommendation. "I came to get a haircut," Janet related. "I left with a haircut and a new friend. That was ten years ago. I've been going to Loan's shop ever since that first visit." Janet's love for the Lord spills over into all of her life, so it was natural that she would talk about her faith as she conversed with her hairdresser. "Loan and I talked of so many things," Janet remembered. "We talked about our children, our homes, and the issues of life. I invited her to Coffee Break many times over the years, but she was never able to attend."

Seeds of faith were being planted in Loan's heart, however, and as Janet continued to see Loan, she continued to nurture spiritual life in her new friend. "Whenever I had an opportunity to bring a small gift, I always made certain that it had a spiritual connection," Janet recalled. "Once I gave Loan a flip calendar with Scripture verses, and the next time I came in she had it right on her work space where everyone could see it. That told me she valued my gift and was open to spiritual things."

Janet exemplified the relational qualities required to make a difference in someone's life. She took a genuine interest in Loan, and she didn't abandon the relationship when Loan turned down the invitations to Coffee Break. It takes time for trust to build, and while ten years seems like a long time to us, eternity lasts forever. Over a period of years Janet shared how her life was influenced by her faith, and how she drew strength from the Lord, especially in times of need. Loan listened and the Holy Spirit worked. And at just the right moment, when Loan's heart had been prepared, God drew her to himself.

A personal health crisis led Loan to surrender her life to the Lord. "I needed major surgery," she said. "I was in the hospital for three weeks, and I didn't know if I would live." When Janet heard about Loan's illness she sent a basket filled with items that would encourage Loan and lift her spirits. Janet also promised to pray for Loan. During this period of illness Loan decided it was time to pray to the Lord herself. "I knew Janet and others were praying for me. Now I needed to pray too." When asked if she had ever prayed before, Loan replied, "I prayed in the boat when we were in the water for three days. But then I didn't know who I was praying to. After Janet told me about the Lord, I knew to pray to him."

God heard her prayers. Loan recovered and returned to work. The spark of faith had been ignited, and Loan was eager to know more about God. At the next visit Janet brought her a Vietnamese Bible. "I was her last customer that day," Janet recalled. "Loan peeked in the gift bag and smiled." "Is that what I think it is?" she asked. Janet nodded yes, and Loan continued. "Wait until we are finished, and we will look at it together." Loan opened the Bible. Turning to the book of Genesis, she began to read aloud in Vietnamese. "What does it say?" Janet questioned. "It says, 'Before anything was God was there, and he made everything,'" Loan answered softly.

Now Loan eagerly accepted Janet's renewed invitation to attend Coffee Break. "It was time for me to learn more about God," she said. The truths of God's Word sank deep into her soul, and her faith blossomed and grew rapidly. When she received news that her father in Vietnam had suffered a serious stroke, she asked for prayers from her group. Then she decided to step out in faith and travel to her former homeland to see her family. "I had not been back since the day I left," she said. "But my father did not know about eternal life. He only knew about reincarnation. I wanted to tell him about God and Jesus." Because of restrictions against religious materials, Loan carried only a Vietnamese Bible and a couple of devotional booklets. During the time she had with her family she talked often about God and Jesus. "I told them how they could receive eternal life," she said. "And I left my Vietnamese Bible with many passages highlighted. There was so much for them to understand. I am praying they will believe."

It has been twenty-four years since Loan fled her homeland. At that time she passed through the waters praying to an unknown god. She returned to Vietnam in faith to tell of the God who loves her and hears her prayers. This God is the Creator, the Redeemer, and the Lord of Loan's life.

Prayer

Lord, I acknowledge you as Creator of all things and as my Redeemer. I am humbled that you call me by name, and I am grateful that you have led me through the deep waters in my life. Give me words and courage to tell others that you are my Savior. Amen.

Touching Lives with Love

For I am convinced that neither death nor life, neither angels nor demons, neither the present nor the future, nor any powers, neither height nor depth, nor anything else in all creation, will be able to separate us from the love of God that is in Christ Jesus our Lord.

—Romans 8:38-39

The whir of the vacuum cleaner slowly faded as Margaret unplugged the machine and prepared to put it away. She couldn't help smiling as she wound up the cord, pleased that her morning's work had ended. "This housecleaning job has been wonderful," she said to herself. "It's been a good place to work." Just then her employer, Wilma, called to say the coffee was ready, and they could both take a break. Margaret sat down at the kitchen table and the two women began to chat. They talked and laughed about their children, a dozen between the two of them. They talked about their extended families, and they talked about their faith. Margaret enjoyed these times and marveled that Wilma could share so openly about what she believed. God seemed so real when Wilma talked about him. Margaret often wished she knew God like Wilma did.

Margaret had discovered this housecleaning job through an ad in the paper, and she was grateful for the extra income. Her husband, Miguel, was a field worker, and work was not always consistent. Both Margaret and Miguel traced their heritage to Mexico. Spanish was the language of choice in their home, but because Margaret was raised in the U.S. she was also fluent in English, and she and Wilma conversed easily. Wilma often talked about the Bible study she led at her church. "It's a little like what we're doing right here in the kitchen," Wilma explained. "We enjoy a cup of coffee, and we talk about God. We even call it 'Coffee Break.'" In her heart Margaret wished she could go to something like that, but she worked every day and her family depended on her income.

One week when Margaret came to work Wilma had a favor to ask. Two Spanish-speaking women were coming to the Bible studies at church, and they were struggling with the English materials. Could Margaret translate the questions into Spanish for them? Margaret agreed, and week after week she translated the lessons with the help of her teenage daughters. To understand the questions they worked with the passage from the Bible. In a sense, Margaret and her daughters were having their own Coffee Break at home.

At work Margaret talked of what she was discovering about Jesus as she translated the questions on the gospel of Mark. Slowly her fledgling faith began to grow.

About a year later Margaret became ill with cancer. Fighting the disease meant that she could no longer work, but at last she could go to Coffee Break. There she met the Spanish women for whom she had translated the lessons, she met the group that had prayed for her, and she met Jesus as her Lord. Although her journey to faith had taken some unusual twists and turns, Margaret rejoiced that God had given her the opportunity to know him better. The Coffee Break group ministered to Margaret as she dealt with cancer. And Margaret became a blessing to the others as she shared her new source of strength.

Many Coffee Break groups can testify to the strength their members receive when they share their struggles. By offering their members comfort and support and prayers, Coffee Break groups dispense God's grace. Leaders bring the love of Jesus into hurting situations as they walk alongside their struggling members. And it's often in the midst of a struggle that faith grows best. Margaret learned to trust the Lord, and even though she did not know what her future held, she knew who held her future.

On the day before Margaret had an appointment with her doctor I visited her at home. In spite of extensive treatment the cancer was not in remission, and this meeting with the doctor would be definitive. I spent some time with Margaret and prayed with her. As I left I wanted to say, "Margaret, everything will be fine. The doctor will give you a good report." But those words weren't given to me. What I could tell her was this: "Margaret, you are a child of God, and you have faith in Jesus. Nothing can separate you from his love. He will be with you tomorrow and always."

The next day Margaret and Miguel went to hear the doctor's report. A member of Margaret's Coffee Break group offered to go with them. Marti was a nurse, fluent in Spanish. She would understand the doctor, and she would be able to explain the prognosis to Miguel and Margaret. When I called Marti that night she told me, "The news is not good. The cancer is advanced, and no further treatment is recommended." "How did Margaret and Miguel respond?" I asked. Marti replied, "Miguel took the news very badly. But Margaret turned to him and said in Spanish, 'Miguel, I have two things. I have cancer, and I have God.'"

"I have God." As a child of God, Margaret had the assurance that nothing could separate her from God's love. Cancer couldn't separate her from God, and the results of cancer could not separate her from God. Not long after, Margaret was translated to glory. She left five school-age daughters and her husband, but she left them with a beautiful story—a story she wrote with her life and her death. It's a story of a life that was touched by the love of friends, the love of her Coffee Break group, and the love of Jesus.

"Touching lives with love" is the goal of Coffee Break and Story Hour, and it has been the theme of the stories in this book. They are just a few of the stories of lives that have been changed by the power of the Word and by people who cared enough to share that Word. New stories are being written every day as men, women, and children discover God's love and respond to him in faith and obedience. Each story is powerful, each is significant. No two stories are alike.

Each one of us is writing a story with our life. Has your story been touched by God's love? It can be if you turn to him in faith. Through faith in Christ you become a child of God, and nothing can separate you from his love. That love will enable you to write your story well, for it will be a story of God's grace and forgiveness. As you share the love of God in your life, you touch another life, and a new story is written. When that story is shared more lives are touched with love, as God is glorified and his kingdom is extended.

Touching lives with love. That's what Coffee Break is all about.

Prayer

Thank you, Father, for touching my life with Jesus' love. Thank you that nothing can separate me from that love. Help me to write my life story so that other lives will be touched by your love. In Jesus' name, Amen.

Afterword

Reading the life-changing stories in this book has filled my heart with immense gratitude to God. For thirty years, God has radically changed lives through Coffee Break. Women, children, and entire families have been touched by God's love. They will never be the same. God is at work through his people and his Word.

In reflecting on these years of blessings, I am very aware of the "cloud of witnesses" spoken of in Hebrews 12:1. Pastors Alvin Vander Griend and Neva Evenhouse were cofounders of Coffee Break, but many others have also felt the call to follow in their footsteps. They are part of the living legacy of God's faithfulness.

Neva had the vision for using small group, inductive Bible study to reach women who didn't know Christ. In the beginning, Neva wrote all the Bible study materials herself, provided leadership training, and directed the program. Neva and Al called it Coffee Break to convey a low-key approach. In 1974, when Al and Neva moved from South Holland, Illinois, to Grand Rapids, Michigan, Coffee Break moved with them. And when Neva moved on to new areas of ministry, Laurie Deters was called to serve as director.

For nine years, Coffee Break was blessed by Laurie's gift of organization and her passionate promotion of the ministry. These formative years in Coffee Break's growth were foundational for the expansion that followed. It was Laurie's dream to gather Coffee Break and Story Hour leaders together in an international convention of praise, thanksgiving, and equipping for leadership. She saw that dream come to reality in 1984, when 650 leaders gathered in Chicago for the first biennial convention to celebrate God's blessings through Coffee Break.

Laurie also was instrumental in moving the Coffee Break program into the solid organizational support of Christian Reformed Home Missions in 1982. With the financial commitment, empowerment, and prayer support of Home Missions, Coffee Break was free to grow as God opened doors. Today Coffee Break continues to be a primary vehicle for evangelism in the Christian Reformed Church in North America and beyond.

More than thirty-five different denominations are represented in the nearly 1,050 programs that use Coffee Break for outreach Bible study. As Coffee Break leaders and group members travel, so does Coffee Break. Transplanted leaders have taken Coffee Break to Scotland, Japan, Mexico, China, Korea, and areas between. Coffee Break's Discover Your Bible materials have been translated into Korean. In addition, the Hispanic small group version of Coffee Break, *Sobremesa,* has its own Spanish-language materials. *Sobremesa* continues to grow.

Story Hour, the accompanying program for preschoolers, has been a part of the Coffee Break ministry since its inception. In fact, it was in watching moms drop their little ones off at Story Hour that Neva and Al recognized the window of opportunity for reaching women in the community. As Coffee Break grew, so did Story Hour, and in 1992 Home Missions premiered Little Lambs, a curriculum specifically intended for two- and three-year-olds. In Story Hour and Little Lambs, loving leaders provide quality care for little ones and introduce them to God and his Word while their moms study the Bible in Coffee Break.

Through the years, Coffee Break/Story Hour regional representatives have been part of Coffee Break's "cloud of witnesses." It has been my privilege to work with all of them. Each has been God's choice "for such a time as this" (Esther 4:14) during the time she served. Each representative has embodied the essence of Coffee Break—devotion to God and God's Word, commitment to prayer, love for people, and a passion for sharing Christ with those who don't know him. They have provided leadership and extended God's grace.

At the beginning of a new millennium, we look forward to a new chapter in the story of Coffee Break, Story Hour, and Little Lambs. If you haven't been a part of the adventure, we invite you to join us, wherever you are on your faith journey.

If you've been touched by the stories you've read and realize you're missing the closeness with God that these women have found, perhaps you would like to attend a Coffee Break Bible study and discover the truths of God's Word for yourself. For information on the Coffee Break nearest you, call 1-888-644-0814.

Or perhaps you're a committed Christian looking for a place to serve. Maybe in reading these stories you've experienced the unmistakable sense that God is calling you to get involved in Coffee Break. If you have a Coffee Break program in your church, please don't hesitate. Call the director of your church program now. On the other hand, there may be no Coffee Break near you, and you'll have to start from scratch. Wonderful! Trust God to provide all you need. We'll do what we can to get you started too. For information on starting a Coffee Break program, call 1-800-333-8300.

Or perhaps you're one of the many Christians who are links in the chain that eventually leads lost people to find God. God bless you for your faithfulness! He is using your obedience to him and your passion for sharing his love to make a difference in someone's eternity.

Touching lives with God's love—that's what Coffee Break is all about. Sharing God's love through studying his Word will bring glory to God, and ultimately "at the name of Jesus, every knee should bow . . . and every tongue confess that Jesus Christ is Lord, to the glory of God the Father" (Phil. 2:10-11).

Betty Veldman
International Director
Coffee Break Ministries